PRACTICALITIES

WORKS BY MARGUERITE DURAS
PUBLISHED BY GROVE WEIDENFELD

Destroy, She Said

Four Novels: The Square;
  10:30 on a Summer Night;
  The Afternoon of Mr. Andesmas;
  Moderato Cantabile

Hiroshima Mon Amour

India Song

The Malady of Death

Practicalities

MARGUERITE DURAS

PRACTICALITIES

Marguerite Duras speaks to Jérôme Beaujour

Translated from the French by Barbara Bray

GROVE WEIDENFELD
New York

Published by Grove Weidenfeld
A division of Wheatland Corporation
841 Broadway
New York, NY 10003-4793

Library of Congress Cataloging-in-Publication Data

Duras, Marguerite.
    [Vie matérielle. English]
    Practicalities : Marguerite Duras speaks to Jérôme
Beaujour /
    Marguerite Duras : translated from the French by
Barbara Bray.—
    1st ed.
        p. cm.
    Translation of: La vie matérielle.
    1. Duras, Marguerite—Interviews.   2. Authors,
French—20th century—Interviews.   I. Beaujour,
Jérôme.   II. Title.
PQ2607.U8245Z47713   1990
843'.912—dc20   89-77417
                                                      CIP

ISBN 0-8021-1073-8

Manufactured in the United States of America

Printed on acid-free paper

First Edition

10 9 8 7 6 5 4 3 2 1

CONTENTS

Contents

PRACTICALITIES

This book helped us pass the time. From the beginning of autumn to the end of winter. All the pieces in it, with very few exceptions, were spoken aloud to Jérôme Beaujour. Then the spoken texts were transcribed, we read them over and appraised them, I made corrections, and Jérôme Beaujour read the result. It was difficult at first. We soon abandoned questions and answers. We tried a subject-by-subject approach, but gave that up too. The last phase of the work consisted of my shortening and lightening the texts and toning them down. It was all done by common consent. As a result of the method we evolved, none of the pieces deals with a topic exhaustively. And none reflects my general views about a particular subject: I don't have general views about anything, except social injustice. At most the book represents what I think sometimes, some days, about some things. So it does incidentally represent what I think. But I don't drag the millstone of totalitarian, i.e., inflexible, thought around with me. That's one plague I've managed to avoid.

The book has no beginning or end, and it hasn't got a middle either. If it's true that every book must have a raison d'être, *this isn't a book at all. Nor is it a journal, or journalism – it doesn't concern itself with ordinary events. Let's just say it's a book intended to be read. Very different from a novel, though its writing was closer to that of a novel – strangely enough, seeing it started out orally – than* to the composing of an editorial. *I had doubts about publishing it in this form, but no previous or current genre could have accommodated such a free kind of writing, these return journeys between you and me, and between myself and myself, in the time we went through together.*

MARGUERITE DURAS

THE SMELL OF CHEMICALS

In 1986 I'll have been in Trouville from the middle of June until the middle of October – longer than the summer. Whenever I'm away from Trouville I feel I've lost the light. Not only the direct bright light of the sun but also the diffused white light of overcast skies and the dark grey light of storms. If I'm away at the end of summer I miss the skies, those long-haul travellers of skies, that come up from beneath the Atlantic. If I'm away in the autumn I miss the haze of high tide, the wind, the oily miasmas of Le Havre, the smell of chemicals. If you get up early you can see a perfect projection of the Black Rocks slanting slightly to the north over the empty beach. Then as the hours go by the shadow shortens and finally disappears.

For years I've moved back and forth between the three houses, at Neauphle-le-Château, Trouville and Paris. For ten years, not wanting to leave Neauphle, I didn't go to Trouville. I even let the place there for a few summers to cover the high running costs. All those years I lived on my own at Neauphle-le-Château, which is why for a long time I didn't get to know anyone at the Black Rocks Hotel. If I spent the summer in any one place it was usually Neauphle, where I knew the whole village.

3

I've never been anywhere where I felt comfortable. I've always been hanging about looking for somewhere or for something to do; I've never been where I wanted to be, except perhaps some summers at Neauphle, in a sort of happy woe. The enclosed garden in *The Atlantic Man*, the despair of loving him – it all happened in that now untended garden. I can still see myself there, closed in on myself, trapped in the ice of the deserted grounds.

I'm the sort of person who's never on time for meals, appointments, the cinema, the theatre, aeroplanes – I always arrive at the last minute. Because I don't trust myself I've taken to getting to the theatre an hour early. I'm delighted when I see other people rush in afraid of being late. I've always turned up on the beach just as everyone else is leaving. I've never acquired a tan because I loathe sunbathing and having sand on my skin and in my hair. I have got brown, though, driving the car or walking in Spain or Italy.

Yet for a considerable part of my life I longed to be able to sunbathe. It went on for ages. I used to work out systems for doing the same as everyone else. That's how, much to my chagrin, I used to be always late. I did what everyone else did, I went on the beach – but in the evening. I did things by halves, just in order to have done them at all, and it didn't work. I very much regret having been like that – obeying the rules but never getting any satisfaction out of it. At the end of the summer I'd feel like an idiot who doesn't know what's been happening, and only knows it's too late to find out. But there is one thing I'm good at, and that's looking at the sea. Not many people have written about the sea as I did in *Summer 1980*. But that's the point: the sea in *Summer 1980* is something I never experienced myself. It's something that

4

happened to me but that I never experienced, something I put into a book precisely because I couldn't have lived it. Always, all my life, that thing about time passing. All my whole life long.

I could have gone on after *Summer 1980*. Just doing that. Keeping a journal of time and the sea – of the rain, the tides, the wind, the rough wind that blows away beach umbrellas and awnings and swirls round the bodies of children in hollows on the beach, and inside the walls of hotels. With time at a standstill in front of me, and the great barrier of the cold, the Arctic winter. But *Summer 1980* remains the only journal I have ever kept. Telling how I was shipwrecked, near to the sea but on land, in the bleak summer of 1980.

THE LADIES OF
THE BLACK ROCKS

Every afternoon here during the summer a number of ladies already getting on in years meet on the terrace of the Black Rocks Hotel and talk. We call them the Ladies of the Black Rocks. Every day, every afternoon of all the summer. But of course you can talk about your life your whole life long; a life is no small matter. The ladies talk on the terrace overlooking the sea until dusk, when it starts to get cool. Other people, passing by, often stop to listen. Sometimes the ladies ask them to stay and join them. The ladies tell about things that have happened to them in their lives, and about things that have happened to other people in other lives, and they are marvellous at it. They've been there for forty years, perched on the débris of the war, talking about central Europe. Some people come every year to this big hotel on the Channel coast. Just to talk.

The ladies would have been between twenty and thirty-five in 1940. Some of them live in Passy. Ladies – the word has no meaning unless you know the ladies of the *département* called 'the Channel', the Ladies of the Black Rocks.

In summer they rebuild Europe out of their networks of friendships, acquaintances, and social and diplomatic connections; out of balls in Vienna and Paris; out of people who died in Auschwitz; out of exile.

Proust used to come to this hotel sometimes. Some of the ladies must have met him. He had Room 111, overlooking the sea. It's as if Swann were still here in the corridors. And it's when the ladies are little girls again that Swann walks.

THE MOTORWAY OF THE WORD

In this sort-of-a-book which isn't really a book at all I'd have liked to talk about this and that, as one does all the time on an ordinary day just like any other. To drive along the motorway of the word, slowing down or stopping as I felt inclined, for no particular reason. But it's impossible – you can't get away from the road itself and the way it's going; you can't not go anywhere; you can't just talk without starting out from a particular point of knowledge or ignorance, and arrive somewhere at random amid the welter of other words. You can't simultaneously know and not know. And so this book, which I'd have liked to resemble a motorway going in all directions at once, will merely be a book that tries to go everywhere but goes to just one place at a time; which turns back and sets out again the same as everyone else, the same as every other book. The only alternative is to say nothing. But that can't be written down.

THE THEATRE

I hope to be able to get out of the house this winter and produce some theatre that's read, not acted. Acting doesn't bring anything to a text. On the contrary, it detracts from it – lessens its immediacy and depth, weakens its muscles and dilutes its blood. That's what I think today. But I think it often. Deep down, that's how I really see the theatre. However, as that kind of theatre doesn't exist, I've tended to forget and go back to thinking about the usual kind. But since the experiment at the Théâtre du Rond-Point in January 1985, I've thought what I'm saying now. Absolutely; once and for all.

An actor reading a book aloud, as in *Blue Eyes, Black Hair*, has nothing else to do but be still and bring the text out of the book by means of the voice alone. No need to gesticulate to show how the body is suffering because of the words being uttered: the whole drama resides in the words themselves and the body remains unmoved. I don't know of any theatrical utterance as powerful as that of the officiants at the various kinds of mass. The Pope's people speak and sing in a curious flat language in which every syllable is given equal weight, without tonic or any other accent; and yet there's nothing to compare with it in either theatre or opera. In the recitatives in the St John and St Matthew Passions, and in Stravinsky's

9

Noces and *Symphony of Psalms* there are similar acoustic dimensions, seemingly newly created, in which the full resonance of the words is heard as it never is in ordinary life. That's what I believe in. Only that. In Gruber's *Bérénice*, which was almost without movement, I didn't like the rudiments of motion that remained – they distanced the words. Bérénice's laments, even conveyed by a great actress like Ludmilla Michaël, didn't have the acoustic dimension they deserved. Why do people still fool themselves about it? Bérénice and Titus are narrators; Racine is the director; the audience is humanity. Why play it in a drawing room or a boudoir? I don't care what anyone thinks about what I've been saying. Give me a theatre to have *Bérénice* read in, and they'll see. The beginnings of what I'm saying now lie in the conversation between the young lovers in *Savannah Bay*, what I've called the 'reported voices'. Something strange happened when the play was done in The Hague – something never achieved by my own two dear actresses. They held the whole theatre with their eyes, they just gazed at the audience, yet they showed what *can* happen in the theatre when the story of the lovers is merely related.

No play by a woman had been performed at the Comédie Française since 1900, nor at Vilar's TNP, nor at the Odéon, nor at Villeurbanne, nor at the Schaubühne, nor at Strehler's Piccolo Teatro. Not one woman playwright or one woman director. And then Sarraute and I began to be performed by the Barraults. George Sand's plays were produced in Paris, but for seventy, eighty, ninety years no play by a woman had been performed there or perhaps in the whole of Europe. I found that out for myself. No one ever told me. And yet it was there for all to see. And then one day I got a letter from Jean-Louis Barrault asking if I'd adapt my long short story, *Days in the Trees*, for the stage. I agreed. The adaptation was rejected by the censors. The play wasn't performed until 1965. It was a great success. But none of the critics pointed out that it was the first play by a woman to be performed in France for nearly a century.

THE LAST CUSTOMER
AT NIGHT

The road went through the Auvergne – the Cantal area. We'd
set out from Saint-Tropez in the afternoon and driven through
part of the night. I can't quite remember what year it was,
but it was in the summer. I'd known him since the beginning
of the year. I'd met him at a dance I'd gone to on my own.
But that's another story. He insisted on stopping before dawn
in Aurillac. The telegram had been delayed – sent to Paris,
then on from there to Saint-Tropez. The funeral was to take
place late the next afternoon. We made love in the hotel in
Aurillac, then made love again. And again the next morning.
I think it was then, on that journey, that that particular desire
emerged clearly in my mind. Because of him, I think. But I'm
not quite sure. But yes, it probably was because of him,
because he had it too, the same desire. But it could have been
anyone. At random, like the last customer at night. We'd had
hardly any sleep, but we set out again very early. It was a
lovely drive, but terribly long, with bends every hundred
yards. Yes, it was on that journey. It's never happened to me
again. The place was ready. On the body. In the hotel rooms.
On the sandy banks of the river. At night. It was in the
châteaux, too, in their walls. In the cruelty of the chase. And
of men. In fear. In the forest. In the wilderness of the rides

through the forest, the lakes, the sky. We took a room by the river. We made love again. We couldn't speak to one another any more. We drank. He struck me, in cold blood. In the face. And parts of the body. We couldn't be near one another now without fear and trembling. He drove me through the grounds and left me at the entrance to the château. The people from the undertaker's were there, and the wardens of the château, and my mother's housekeeper and my elder brother. My mother hadn't been put in her coffin yet. They were all waiting for me. My mother. I kissed the cold forehead. My brother was crying. There were only three of us at the church in Ozain, the wardens of the château had stayed behind. I thought about the man waiting for me in the hotel by the river. I didn't feel any grief for the dead woman, or for the man who was weeping, her son. I've never felt any since. Afterwards there was the meeting with the solicitor. I agreed to everything it said in my mother's will; I disinherited myself.

He was waiting for me in the grounds. We slept in the hotel by the Loire. We lingered on by the river for a few days. We used to stay in our room till late afternoon. We drank. We went out and drank. Then came back to the room. Then went out again at night. Looking for cafés that were still open. It was madness. We couldn't tear ourselves away from the place, from the river. We didn't speak of what was in our minds. Sometimes we were afraid. We were overwhelmed with grief. We wept. But the word was never spoken. We were sorry we didn't love one another. We couldn't remember anything. That's what we said. We knew it would never happen to us again, but we never referred to it, nor to the fact that we were both faced with the same strange desire. The madness lasted the whole winter. After that it became less important – just a love affair. And after that again, I wrote *Moderato Cantabile*.

ALCOHOL

I've spent whole summers at Neauphle alone except for drink. People used to come on the weekends. But during the week I was alone in that huge house, and that was how alcohol took on its full significance. It lends resonance to loneliness, and ends up making you prefer it to everything else. Drinking isn't necessarily the same as wanting to die. But you can't drink without thinking you're killing yourself. Living with alcohol is living with death close at hand. What stops you killing yourself when you're intoxicated out of your mind is the thought that once you're dead you won't be able to drink any more. I started drinking at parties and political meetings – glasses of wine at first, then whisky. And then, when I was forty-one, I met someone who really loved alcohol and drank every day, though sensibly. I soon outstripped him. That went on for ten years, until I got cirrhosis of the liver and started vomiting blood. Then I gave up drinking for ten years. That was the first time. Then I started again, and gave it up again, I forget why. Then I stopped smoking, but I could only do that by drinking again. This is the third time I've given it up. I've never smoked opium or hash. I 'doped' myself with aspirin every day for fifteen years, but I've never taken drugs. At first I drank whisky and Calvados – what I call the pale kinds of alcohol. And beer, and vervain from Velay – they say that's the worst for the liver. Lastly I started to drink wine, and I never stopped.

I became an alcoholic as soon as I started to drink. I drank like one straight away, and left everyone else behind. I began by drinking in the evening, then at midday, then in the morning, and then I began to drink at night. First once a night, then every two hours. I've never drugged myself any other way. I've always known that if I took to heroin it would soon get out of control. I've always drunk with men. Alcohol is linked to the memory of sexual violence – it makes it glow, it's inseparable from it. But only in the mind. Alcohol is a substitute for pleasure though it doesn't replace it. People obsessed with sex aren't usually alcoholics. Alcoholics, even those in the gutter, tend to be intellectuals. The proletariat, a class far more intellectual now than the bourgeoisie, has a propensity for alcohol, as can be seen all over the world. Of all human occupations, manual work is probably the kind that leads most directly to thought, and therefore to drink. Just look at the history of ideas. Alcohol makes people talk. It's spirituality carried to the point where logic becomes lunacy; it's reason going mad trying to understand why this kind of society, this Reign of Injustice, exists. And it always ends in despair. A drunk is often coarse, but rarely obscene. Sometimes he loses his temper and kills. When you've had too much to drink you're back at the start of the infernal cycle of life. People talk about happiness, and say it's impossible. But they know what the word means.

What they lack is a god. The void you discover one day in your teens – nothing can ever undo that discovery. But alcohol was invented to help us bear the void in the universe

– the motion of the planets, their imperturbable wheeling through space, their silent indifference to the place of our pain. A man who drinks is interplanetary. He moves through interstellar space. It's from there he looks down. Alcohol doesn't console, it doesn't fill up anyone's psychological gaps, all it replaces is the lack of God. It doesn't comfort man. On the contrary, it encourages him in his folly, it transports him to the supreme regions where he is master of his own destiny. No other human being, no woman, no poem or music, book or painting can replace alcohol in its power to give man the illusion of real creation. Alcohol's job is to replace creation. And that's what it does do for a lot of people who ought to have believed in God and don't any more. But alcohol is barren. The words a man speaks in the night of drunkenness fade like the darkness itself at the coming of day. Drunkenness doesn't create anything, it doesn't enter into the words, it dims and slackens the mind instead of stimulating it. I've spoken under its influence. The illusion's perfect: you're sure what you're saying has never been said before. But alcohol can't produce anything that lasts. It's just wind. I've written under its influence too – I had the knack of keeping tipsiness at bay, probably because I have such a horror of it. I never drank in order to get drunk. I never drank fast. I drank all the time and I was never drunk. I was withdrawn from the world – inaccessible but not intoxicated.

When a woman drinks it's as if an animal were drinking, or a child. Alcoholism is scandalous in a woman, and a female alcoholic is rare, a serious matter. It's a slur on the divine in our nature. I realized the scandal I was causing around me. But in my day, in order to have the strength to con-front it publicly – for example, to go into a bar on one's own at night – you needed to have had something to drink already.

It's always too late when people tell someone they drink too much. 'You drink too much.' But it's a shocking thing to say whenever you say it. You never know yourself that you're an alcoholic. In a hundred per cent of cases it's taken as an insult. The person concerned says, 'You're only saying that to get at me.' In my own case the disease had already taken hold by the time I was told about it. We live in a world paralysed with principles. We just let other people die. I don't think this kind of thing happens with drugs. Drugs cut the addict off completely from the rest of humanity. But they don't throw him to the winds or into the street; they don't turn him into a vagabond. But alcohol means the gutter, the dosshouse, other alcoholics. With drugs it's very quick: death comes fast – speechlessness, darkness, closed shutters, help-lessness. Nor is there any consolation for stopping drinking. Since I've stopped I feel for the alcoholic I once was. I really did drink a lot. Then help came – but now I'm telling my own story instead of talking about alcohol in general. It's incredibly simple – for real alcoholics there's probably the simplest possible explanation. They're in a place where suffering can't hurt them. *Clochards* aren't unhappy, it's silly to say that when they're drunk from morn till night, twenty-four hours a day. They couldn't lead the life they lead anywhere else but in the street. During the winter of 1986-7 they preferred to risk dying of cold rather than go into a hostel and give up their litre of *rouge*. Everyone tried to work out why they wouldn't go into the dosshouse. That was the reason.

The night hours aren't the worst. But of course that's the

most dangerous time if you suffer from insomnia. You mustn't have a drop of alcohol in the house. I'm one of those alcoholics who can be set off again by drinking just one glass of wine. I don't know the medical term for it.

An alcoholic's body is like a telephone exchange, like a set of different compartments all linked together. It's the brain that's affected first. The mind. First comes happiness through the mind. Then through the body. It's lapped around, saturated, then borne along – yes, that's the word for it, borne along. And after a time you have the choice – whether to keep drinking until you're senseless and lose your identity, or to go no further than the beginnings of happiness. To die, so to speak, every day, or to go on living.

THE PLEASURES OF
THE 6th ARRONDISSEMENT

I've missed out on the pleasures of the 6th arrondissement which people talk about all over the world.

I may have been to the Tabou once – perhaps twice, but I don't think so. I've cast an eye at the Deux Magots and the Flore, but not very often. As soon as I'd made *Hiroshima* and people started recognizing me, that was it – I steered clear of those fearful terraces. (I used to go to Lipp's because of Fernandez. And I have been to the Quatre Saisons.)

Why?

Pride. I was too short to go to places where the women were tall. I wore the same clothes every day. I had just the one dress, black and all-purpose, dating from the war. I was self-conscious, as young people often are, at not being 'in the swim'. All in all, for various reasons, my whole life's been overcast by that sort of shame.

It's soon too late in life to go to the Tabou or the Deux Magots. It was soon all over – public places, dancing. In my day. For women, I mean.

VINH LONG

There was Vinh Long, and there was Hanoi. I've talked about
Vinh Long already, but never about Hanoi. As I've said
before, Vinh Long was an outpost in Cochin China. You're
already on the Plain of Birds there, the biggest irrigated
landscape in the world, I should think. I was between eight
and ten years old when it happened. Like a thunderbolt, or
faith. It affected my whole life. I'm seventy-two now, but it's
still as though it were yesterday: the paths there in the
afternoon when everyone was asleep, the White quarter, the
empty streets with their rows of flame-trees. The sleeping
river. And her going by in her black limousine. Her name
is almost Anne-Marie Stretter. Her name is Striedter. The
governor's wife. They've got two children. They came here
from Laos; she had a young lover there. He's just killed
himself because she went away. It's all there, as in *India Song*.
The young man stayed on in Laos, the post where they'd
met, away up north on the Mekong. He killed himself there.
In Luang Prabang.

First there was Vinh Long, through which the river linking
the lovers flowed, a thousand kilometres farther downstream.
I can remember what my childish body felt: as if some

knowledge had been vouchsafed to it that was still forbidden. The world was huge and complex yet very clear. One would have to invent a word for it – for the way I managed to act as if I didn't understand what was there to be understood. I couldn't talk about it to anyone, not even my mother – I knew she lied to us children about such things. I had to keep the knowledge entirely to myself. From then on Anne-Marie Stretter was my secret.

HANOI

And there was Hanoi too, which I've never talked about, I don't know why. Before Vinh Long, six years before, there was Hanoi. In the house my mother had bought on the Little Lake. At that time my mother took in paying guests. Vietnamese and Laotian boys aged about twelve or thirteen. One afternoon one of them asked me to go with him to a 'hidey-hole'. I wasn't afraid, so I went. The place was on the edge of the lake, between a couple of wooden huts that must have belonged to the house. I can remember a kind of narrow passage between walls made of planks. This was where the defloration in the book took place: among the bathing huts. The lake became the sea, but the pleasure was there even then, its nature already essentially foreshadowed. And also unforgettable even then, in the body of a child light-years away from understanding what it was, but already receiving the signal, even then. The next day my mother sent the Vietnamese boy packing – I'd thought it my duty to tell her everything, confess everything. I can remember it all quite plainly. It is as if I was dishonoured by having been touched. I was four years old. He was eleven and a half – not yet pubescent. His prick was still limp and soft. He told me what to do. I took hold of it, he put his hand on mine, and our two hands stroked it more and more strongly. Then he stopped. I've never forgotten the feel of its shape in my hand, or its warmth. Or the child's face, eyes shut, martyr-like, waiting for, straining towards, a pleasure still out of reach.

I never mentioned it to my mother again. For the rest of her life she thought I'd forgotten. She'd said, 'You must never think about it again. Never, ever.' For a long while I did think about it, though, as about something terrible. I only spoke of it much later, to men in France. But I knew my mother had never forgotten those childish pranks.

The scene shifted of its own accord. It grew up with me, in fact, and has never left me.

THE BLACK BLOCK

When you're writing, a kind of instinct comes into play. What you're going to write is already there in the darkness. It's as if writing were something outside you, in a tangle of tenses: between writing and having written, having written and having to go on writing; between knowing and not knowing what it's all about; starting from complete meaning, being submerged by it, and ending up in meaninglessness. The image of a black block in the middle of the world isn't far out.

It isn't the transition Aristotle speaks of, from potential to actual being. It isn't a translation. It's not a matter of passing from one state to another. It's a matter of deciphering something already there, something you've already done in the sleep of your life, in its organic rumination, unbeknown to you. It isn't something 'transferred' – that's not it. It might be that the instinct I referred to is the power of reading before it's written something that's still illegible to everyone else. I could put it differently. I could say it's the ability to read your own writing, the first stage of your own writing, while it's still indecipherable to others. It's as if you have to regress, condescend towards other people's writing for the book to become legible to them. This could be said in other words again, but it would still amount to the same thing. You have in front of you a mass suspended between life and death and entirely dependent upon you. I've often had this feeling, of a confrontation between something that was already there and something that was about to take its place. I'm in the middle, and I seize the mass that's already there, move it about, smash it up – it's almost a question of muscles, of physical dexterity. You have to move faster than the non-writing part of you, which is always up there on the plane of thought, always threatening to fade out, to disappear into limbo as far as the future story is concerned; the part which will never descend to the level of writing; which refuses all drudgery. But you have the feeling that sometimes the non-writing part of you is asleep, and thereby yields itself up and enters completely into the ordinary aspect of writing that will constitute the book. But between these two states there are many intermediate ones, of differing degrees of felicity. Sometimes you could almost use the word happiness. When I was writing *The Lover* I felt I was *discovering* something: it was there before me, before everything, and would still be there after I'd come to think things were otherwise – that it was mine, that it was there for me. It was more or less as I've described, and the process of writing it down was so smooth it reminded you of the way you speak when you're drunk, when what you say always seems so simple and clear. Then all of a sudden it would start to resist. When that happens you feel as if you're in a sort of carapace – nothing can get through from yourself to yourself, or from yourself to anyone else. How can I convey it, how can I describe the experience, the sense of an almost tragic refusal to go on writing, as if it were impossible. Then, after ten minutes or so, perhaps after I'd interrelated a couple of words, some more lines would begin to emerge.

Writing isn't just telling stories. It's exactly the opposite. It's telling everything at once. It's the telling of a story, and the absence of the story. It's telling a story through its absence. Lol V. Stein is destroyed by the dance at S. Thala. Lol V. Stein is created by the dance at S. Thala.

The Ravishing of Lol Stein is a book apart, the only one of a kind. It separates the readers-cum-writers who've identified with L. V. Stein's madness from those who have not.

I'd like to draw a distinction between what I've said, and said several times, and what I haven't said about the book. Here's what I think I've said: during the actual dance at S. Thala, Lol V. Stein is so carried away by the sight of her fiancé and the stranger in black that she forgets to suffer. She doesn't suffer at having been forgotten and betrayed. It's because her suffering is suppressed that she later goes mad. You could put it differently and say that she realizes her fiancé is being drawn towards another woman, and she completely identifies with this decision, although it's against herself; and it's because of this that she loses her reason. It's a kind of oblivion. Like a phenomenon related to the freezing of water. Water turns to ice at zero degrees, but sometimes, when the weather's very cold, the air is so still that the water *forgets* to freeze. It can descend to minus five degrees and freeze only then.

What I haven't said is that all the women in my books, whatever their age, derive from Lol V. Stein. Derive, that is, from a kind of self-forgetting. They all see quite clearly and lucidly. But they're imprudent, improvident. They all ruin their own lives. They're very timid, they're afraid of streets and public places, they don't expect to be happy. The women in all these books and films are alike, the whole procession of them, from *The Woman from the Ganges* to the last version of Lol V. Stein in the script that got lost. Where did I get the idea for that script from? I forget. It was just like one of the hallucinations I used to get after I had the drying-out treatment.

It took place in a town. The casino was lit up, and the same dance was in progress, as if it had been going on for twenty years. Yes, I think that was it. It's a repetition of the dance at S. Thala, but treated dramatically. You don't get to know any more about Lol V. Stein – that's all over and done with. Now she's going to die. She's stopped haunting me, she lets me alone, I kill her, I kill her so that she'll stop getting in my way, lying down in front of my houses, my books, sleeping on the beaches in all weathers, in the wind and the cold, waiting, waiting for this – for me to look at her again for the last time. Her madness is famous; she's old; she's carried out of the casino in a chair; she's Chinese now. The chair is carried by porters – on their shoulders, like a coffin. She's heavily made up. She doesn't know what's going on. She looks at the people, the town. Her hair is dyed, she's painted like a whore, she's utterly destroyed – or, as you might say, born. She has become the most beautiful sentence I ever wrote: 'It's S. Thala here as far as the river, and beyond the river it's S. Thala still.'

Thala's the word that's cried out on the top floor of the Black Rocks Hotel by the young stranger with blue eyes, black hair.

A few days ago a friend of mine just back from Rio de Janeiro said to me: 'Would you believe it? Lol V. Stein, that book of ours that's so difficult – the first thing I saw there was "O Deslumbramento 5 Edição" all lit up in the windows of the airport bookshops.'

Lol V. Stein.
Mad.
Brought to a halt at the dance at S. Thala. She stops there. It's the dance that grows, making concentric circles round her, bigger and bigger. Now the dance, the sound of the dance, has reached as far as New York. Now, of all the characters in my books, Lol V. Stein comes top of the list. It's a funny thing. She's the one who 'sells' the best. My little madwoman.

BONNARD

No, it wasn't a Monet or a Manet. It was a Bonnard. It was at the house of some people in Berne who were great art collectors. They had a painting by Bonnard: a boat, with the wife's family in it. Bonnard always wanted to alter the sail, and because he kept on about it they let him have the painting back. When he returned it he said he considered it finished now. But the sail had swallowed up everything, dwarfing the sea, the people in the boat and the sky. That can happen with a book: you can start a new sentence and change the whole subject. You don't notice anything; you look up at the window and it's evening. And the next morning you find you've sat down to a different book. The making of pictures and books isn't something completely conscious. And you can never, never find words for it.

THE BLUE OF THE SCARF

I'm the only one who knows what kind of blue the girl in the book's scarf is. That doesn't matter – but there are other inadequacies that do. For example, I'm also the only one who can see her smile and the look in her eyes. But I know I shall never be able to describe them to you. Make you – or anyone else, ever – see them too.

And some things remain unknown even to the author. In my case, some of the things Lol V. Stein does, some of the risks she takes, at the party she gives where Tatiana Karl and others play billiards. A distant violin is heard somewhere in the house. It's Lol's husband playing. Her attitude – the secret understanding between her and Jacques Hold during dinner, which changed the book's ending – I can't translate it or convey its meaning because I'm completely with Lol V. Stein and she herself doesn't quite know what she's doing or why. Blanchot has criticized me for using someone like Jacques Hold as an intermediary, in order to get close to her. He'd have preferred there to be no intermediary. But I can only get to grips with her when she's engaged in some action with another character; when I can see her and hear her. She's never hand-to-hand with me, like the Vice-Consul. A piece of writing is a whole that proceeds as a whole – it never presents itself as a matter of choice. Even if I find at the end of a book that one of the characters really loved a certain other character and not the one I've indicated, I don't alter the book's past, which is already written – I alter its future. When I myself notice the love isn't what I thought, I'm with the new love, I start off again with it. I don't say the love that's abandoned was wrong; I say it's dead. After the dinner at LVS's the colours remain the same, the colours of the walls and those in the garden. No one knows yet what is just about to change.

I've talked a lot about writing. But I don't know what it is.

MEN

If you have a mind to generalize you might say *The Malady of Death* is a preliminary version of *Blue Eyes, Black Hair*. But *The Malady of Death* is an indictment, and there's nothing at all like that in the longer book.

Other people, from Peter Handke to Maurice Blanchot, have seen *The Malady of Death* as being against men in their relationship with women. If you like. But I say if men have taken such an interest in the book it's because they've sensed there's something more to it than that – something of particular concern to them. It's extraordinary that they should have seen it. But it's also extraordinary that some of them haven't seen that in *The Malady of Death*, as well as a man in relation to women, and seen through that, there's a man in relation to men.

The men are homosexuals. All men are potentially homosexuals – all that's missing is awareness of the fact, an incident or revelation that will bring it home to them. Homosexuals themselves know this and say so. And women who've known homosexuals and really loved them know it and say so too.

The covert queer – loud, intrusive, delightful, a favourite

everywhere – bears witness at the very centre of both his body and his mind to the death of the organic, fraternal contradiction between men and women; to the absolute disappearance of woman as a secondary element.

The book is not so much the result of an actual experience as an intuition, a kind of blinding perception of what really goes on among men. It isn't due to a personal knowledge of men and of their general condition – it's self-evident. But I don't apply words to it any more. Now that I know it I no longer have the words to say it. It's just there, and it can't be named any more. You can proceed from a distance, using metaphor to get closer if you like. But I don't say now what I said before, in *The Malady of Death*. What I say now is this: it's a difference residing in one word, but no one knows which; residing in the depth of a shadow over a word, in the way it's said. All of a sudden a colour that's ordinary, a blue that's ugly. Only a slight difference, but conclusive. Or perhaps, on the other hand though equally likely, the absence of a shadow – everywhere, on land and sea. And in the eyes the gentle glaze that comes from lack of love.

It's between men and women that imagination is at its strongest. And it's there that they're separated by a frigidity which women increasingly invoke and which paralyses the men who desire them. The woman herself usually doesn't know what the malady is that's depriving her of desire. Much oftener than is generally supposed she doesn't know what desire is, how it manifests itself in women. She thinks there are things she has to do in order to feel it as other women do. There's nothing to be said about this, except that wherever you think imagination is absent, that's where it's at its most powerful. In frigidity. Frigidity is desire imagined by a woman who doesn't desire the man offering himself to her. It's the desire of a woman for a man who hasn't yet come to her, whom she doesn't yet know. She's faithful to this stranger even before she belongs to him. Frigidity is the non-desire for whatever is not him. And the end of frigidity is something unpredictable and infinite – a man can't altogether keep up with it. It's the desire a woman feels for her lover alone. Whatever he's like, whatever social class he belongs to, he will become her lover if it's him she desires. This inescapable vocation for just one being in the whole world is a feminine characteristic. It can happen with heterosexual lovers that desire attaches to just the one person for both of them, and the man, like the woman, becomes frigid or impotent if they change partners. But it happens much less often with men. Even if these notions are rather sweeping and depressing, they're the ones that come closest to the truth.

Heterosexuality is dangerous. It tempts you to aim at a perfect duality of desire.

In heterosexual love there's no solution. Man and woman are irreconcilable, and it's the doomed attempt to do the impossible, repeated in each new affair, that lends heterosexual love its grandeur.

But in homosexual love the passion is homosexuality itself. What a homosexual loves, as if it were his lover, his country, his art, his land, is homosexuality.

Desire for our lover hits us in the vaginal cavity, which reverberates like an echo chamber within our bodies. A place from which our lover's penis is absent. We can't deceive ourselves – can't imagine another penis in the place meant for just one man, the one who's our lover. If another man touches us we cry out in disgust. We possess our lover just as he possesses us. We possess each other. And the site of the possession is one of absolute subjectivity. It's there our lover deals us the strongest blows, which we implore him to deal so that they may echo all through our body and through our emptying mind. It's there that we want to die.

A writer who hasn't known women, has never touched a woman's body and perhaps never read any books or poems written by women, and yet thinks he's been involved in literature, is mistaken. You can't be ignorant of such essential data and still be an intellectual leader, even just for your peers. Although I felt quite friendly towards Roland Barthes I could never admire him. He always struck me as very careful and professorial, and strictly partisan. After the 'Mythologies' series I couldn't read him any more. I tried after he died to read his book on photography, but again I couldn't get on with it, except for a very fine chapter about his mother. The much revered mother who had been his companion, and the only heroine in the wilderness of his life. Then I tried to read *A Lover's Discourse: Fragments*, but I couldn't. Obviously it's very clever. Jottings on love – yes, on love, but in making them he managed in fact not to love at all, as far as I can see. A charming man, really charming, of course. And a writer, of course. That's the point. A writer of writing that's stiff and regular.

Even if they belong to some religious sect, people need to

open up to the unknown – let it come in and stir things up! We also need to open up the law and leave it open, so that something can come in and upset the usual mechanisms of liberty. We need to open up to what's impious and what's forbidden, so that the unknown element in things may enter and be seen. Roland Barthes must have gone straight from childhood to adulthood without ever passing through the dangers of adolescence.

Men often interpret the sexual passages in my books as due to prejudice on my part. They pick over everything they read, everything we do. And laugh at any sexuality not their own.

Some men have been repelled by the couple in *The Lover* – the little white girl and the Chinese lover. They skip some pages, they say, or shut their eyes. Shut their eyes while they're reading! To them *The Lover*'s just the crazy family, the drives, the ferry, Saigon by night and the whole colonial caboodle. But not the little White and her Chinese lover. On the other hand, the couple in *The Lover* fills most men with a strange desire – one that rises up from the mists of time and the depths of humanity: the desire of incest and rape. For me that little girl walking through the town as if she were on her way to high school, but really, as she goes along the vast boulevard full of trams, through streets and markets crowded with people, making her way towards the man, towards her slavish obligation towards her lover – she has a freedom I myself have lost.

I can remember the feeling of hands on bodies, and the coolness of the water out of the jars. I can remember the heat;

such heat is unimaginable now. I'm the one who lets herself be washed; he doesn't dry my body; he carries me, still wet, over to the camp bed – the wood smooth as silk, and cool – and switches on the fan. He devours me with a strength and gentleness that shatter me.

The skin. My little brother's skin. It's the same. And the hand. The same.

I think men's behaviour to women is generally brutal and high-handed. But that doesn't necessarily mean men are brutal and high-handed – only that men are like that in the context of the heterosexual couple. Because they are uneasy in that relationship. They act a part, because they're bored. In a heterosexual couple the man is biding his time – his own time. He doesn't know he's doing it. The number of men in heterosexual couples (or in drawing rooms or on beaches or in the streets) who are just waiting, all alone, with no language in common between them and their partners, and don't know it – if you take all the countries in the world it must run into millions and millions. But such men come out of themselves when they drop the role they play in a heterosexual couple. The equivalent of intimate conversation between women is something men experience only with other men. Talking means talking about sex. And talking about sex is part of sex itself. Not at all the same as talking about sport or the office.

It's women who upset the applecart. Between themselves they talk only about the practicalities of life. They're not supposed to enter the realm of the mind. Very few of them are aware of it. A lot of them still haven't found out. For centuries women have been informed about themselves by men, and men tell them they're inferior. But speech is freer in that situation of deprivation and oppression just because it doesn't go beyond the practicalities of life. It's much more ancient, too. For centuries women were merely the vehicles of a more or less inevitable suffering – until it came to light in the first book written about women. It's not men, it's women who are young and fresh. But in the past they didn't know.

The thing that's between us is fascination, and the fascination resides in our being alike. Whether you're a man or a woman, the fascination resides in finding out that we're alike.

If you're a man your favourite company – that of your heart, your flesh and your sex – is the company of men. And it's in this context that you approach women. It's the other man, man number two inside you, who lives with your wife and has sexual relations with her – ordinary sexual relations which may be utilitarian, gastronomical, vital, amorous, or even passionate, and which also produce children and families. But the chief man inside you, man number one, has real relationships with men, his brothers. You listen to your wives' restful conversations as a whole, not in detail, as if they were just old refrains. One doesn't listen to women, doesn't pay any attention to what they say. But we're not blaming you for that. Women do tend to be boring still, and a lot of them haven't the nerve to step out of line. Nor would you want them to. The French bourgeoisie would like women to go on being treated as minors. But now women know what's what. And they're quitting, they're leaving men; and they're much happier than they used to be. Each one used to be acting a part with her man. Though much less so in the case of homosexuals, even then.

A man's transition from heterosexuality to homosexuality involves a very severe crisis. No change could possibly be greater. The man doesn't know himself any more. It's as if he were being born. In most cases he can't control or understand the crisis. He doesn't recognize what's happening, for a start, because of course he rejects the possibility that he might be a homosexual. As for his wife, she knows, whether she finds out from him or from others, including women friends. She begins to 'realize' everything. She sees all he's done or said in the past in a new light. She says, 'It must have been there all the time and he didn't see it. And he, together with everyone else, has suddenly found out.'

It will be the greatest disaster ever. At first it will only be below the surface. A slight fall in the population. People won't work any more. There'll be massive immigration to ensure that things get done. And then no one will know what to do. Perhaps everyone will just wait for the population to dwindle away. They'd sleep all the time. The death of the last man would pass unnoticed. But maybe some more heterosexuals would turn up and begin the game all over again.

Yes, it really is difficult to talk about sex. Before they're plumbers or writers or taxi drivers or unemployed or journalists, before everything else, men are men. Whether heterosexual or homosexual. The only difference is that some of them remind you of it as soon as you meet them, and others wait for a little while. You have to be very fond of men. Very, very fond. You have to be very fond of them to love them. Otherwise they're simply unbearable.

HOUSE AND HOME

A house means a family house, a place specially meant for putting children and men in so as to restrict their waywardness and distract them from the longing for adventure and escape they've had since time began. The most difficult thing in tackling this subject is to get down to the basic and utterly manageable terms in which women see the fantastic challenge a house represents: how to provide a centre for children and men at one and the same time.

The house a woman creates is a Utopia. She can't help it – can't help trying to interest her nearest and dearest not in happiness itself but in the search for it. As if the search were the point of the whole thing, not something to be rejected out of hand because it's too general. She says you must both understand and be chary of this strange preoccupation with happiness. She thinks this attitude will help the children later on. For that's what a woman, a mother wants – to teach her children to take an interest in life. She knows it's safer for them to be interested in other people's happiness than to believe in their own.

At Neauphle I often used to cook in the early afternoon. That was when no one else was there – when the others were at work, or out for a walk, or asleep in their rooms. Then I had all the ground floor of the house and the garden to myself. It was then I saw most clearly that I loved them and wished them well. I can recall the kind of silence there was after they went out. To enter that silence was like entering the sea. At once a happiness and a very precise state of abandonment to an evolving idea. A way of thinking or perhaps of not thinking – the two things are not so far apart. And also of writing.

Slowly and carefully, so as to make it last, I'd cook, those afternoons, for the people who weren't there. I'd make some soup so that it would be ready for them if they came in very hungry. If no soup was ready there wasn't anything. If nothing was ready it was because there wasn't anything; nobody was there. Often the ingredients were there, bought that morning, and all I had to do was prepare the vegetables, put the soup on, and write.

I thought for a long while about buying a house. I never imagined I could ever own a new one. The house at Neauphle used to be a couple of farms built a little while before the Revolution. It must be just over two hundred years old. I've often thought about it, It was there in 1789 and 1870. It's where the forests of Rambouillet and Versailles meet. And in 1958 it belonged to me. I thought about it some nights till it almost hurt. I saw it lived in by the women. I saw myself as preceded by them, in the same bedrooms, the same twilights. There'd been nine generations of women before me within those walls; dozens of people gathered around the fires – children, farm workers, cow girls. All over the house there were surfaces rubbed smooth where grown-ups, children, and dogs had gone in and out of the doors.

The thing women brood on for years – it's the bed their thoughts flow along while the children are still small – is how to keep them safe from harm. They usually brood in vain.

Some women can never manage it – they can't handle their houses, they overload them, clutter them up, never create an opening towards the world outside. They can't help it, but they get it all wrong and make the house unbearable, so that the children run away as soon as they're fifteen, the same as we did. We ran away because the only adventure left to us was one all worked out by our mothers.

Lots of women never solve the problem of disorder – of the house being overrun by the chaos families produce. They know they'll never be able to overcome the incredible difficulties of keeping a house in order. Though anyhow there's nothing to be done about it. That sort of woman simply shifts disorder from one room to another; moves it about or hides it in cellars, disused rooms, trunks or cupboards. Women like that have locked doors in their own houses that they daren't open, even in front of the family, for fear of being put to shame. Many are willing enough but naïve – they think you can solve the problem of disorder by putting the tidying-up off until later, not realizing their 'later' doesn't exist and never will. And that even if it did come it would be too late. They don't realize that disorder, or in other words the accumulation of possessions, can only be dealt with in a way that's extremely painful. Namely by parting with them. Some families with big houses keep everything for three hundred years – dresses, toys, and anything to do with the children, the squire or the mayor.

I've thrown things away, and regretted it. Sooner or later

you always regret having thrown things away at some time or other. But if you don't part with anything, if you try to hold back time, you can spend your whole life tidying life up and documenting it. Women often keep gas and electricity bills for twenty years, for no other reason than to record time and their own virtues. The time they once had, but of which nothing remains.

I say it again. It bears a lot of repetition. A woman's work, from the time she gets up to the time she goes to bed, is as hard as a day at war, worse than a man's working day. Because she has to make her time-table conform to those of other people – her own family and the various organizations it's connected with.

In a morning five hours long, she gets the children's breakfasts, washes and dresses them, does the housework, makes the beds, washes and dresses herself, does the shopping, does the cooking, lays the table. In twenty minutes she gives the children their lunch, yelling at them the while, then takes them back to school, does the dishes, does the washing, and so on and so on. Maybe, at about half-past three, she gets to read the paper for half an hour.

From the man's point of view a woman is a good mother when she turns this discontinuity into a silent and unobtrusive continuity.

This silent continuity used to be regarded as life itself, not just one of its aspects, the same as work. And now we've got to the root of the matter or the bottom of the mine.

The silent continuity seemed so natural and lasted so long that in the end, for the people around the woman who practised it, it no longer existed at all. To men, women's work was like the rain-bringing clouds, or the rain itself. The task involved was carried out every day as regularly as sleep. So men were happy – men in the Middle Ages, men at the time of the Revolution, and men in 1986: everything in the garden was lovely.

I've forgotten to say one thing that women ought to get into their heads. Don't let anyone tell you different: the sons are no different from the fathers. They treat women just the same way. Cry the same way when one of them dies. Say nothing can ever take her place.

That's how it used to be in the past. In the past, wherever I turn, to whatever point in the history of the world, I see women in an extreme and intolerable situation. Doing a balancing act over death.

Now, whichever way I turn in my own time I see the starlets of the media, tourism and banking, each one the bright girl of the class, spruce and indefatigable, equally knowledgeable about everything. And doing a balancing act over death.

So, you see, I write to no purpose. I write as it seems to me one has to write. For nothing. I don't even write for women. I write about women in order to write about myself, about myself alone through the ages.

I've read Virginia Woolf's *A Room of One's Own*, and Michelet's *The Witch*.

But I don't have books any more. I've got rid of them, and of any idea of having them. It's all over. With those two books it was as if I'd opened up my own body and mind and were reading an account of my own life in the Middle Ages, in the forests, and in the factories of the nineteenth century. But I couldn't find one man who'd read the Woolf book. We're cut off from one another, as M.D. says in her novels.

The mental house and the physical house.

My first school was my mother herself. How she ran her houses. How she did the work. It was she who taught me cleanliness – the thoroughgoing, morbid, superstitious cleanliness of a mother with three young children in Indochina in 1915.

What my mother wanted was to make sure that we, her children, whatever happened, however serious, even war – that we'd never in all our lives be caught unawares. As long as we had a house and our mother, we'd never be abandoned or swept away or taken by surprise. There could be wars, droughts, we might be cut off by floods; but we'd always have a house, a mother, and something to eat and drink. I believe that right up to the end of her life she made jam in preparation for a third war. She stockpiled sugar and pasta. Hers was a kind of gloomy arithmetic derived from a fundamental pessimism which I've inherited in its entirety.

Over the episode of the dykes my mother had been swindled and abandoned by everyone. She brought us up completely unaided. She told us she'd been swindled and abandoned because our father was dead and she was defenceless. One thing she was certain of, and that was that we were all abandoned.

47

I have this deep desire to run a house. I've had it all my life. There's still something of it left. Even now I still have to know all the time what there is to eat in the cupboards, if there's everything that's needed in order to hold out, live, survive. I too still hanker after a sort of shipboard self-sufficiency on the voyage of life for the people I love and for my child.

I often think of the houses my mother had, the ones that went with her various posts. Seven hours' trek along unmade roads from the nearest white settlement and the nearest doctor. The cupboards were always full of food and medicine – gruel, soft soap, alum, acids, vinegars, quinine, disinfectants, Emetine, Peptofer, Pulmoserum, Hepatrol, charcoal. I mean, she wasn't just my mother – she was a kind of institution. The natives used to come to her too, for treatment. A house is that too – it overflows. That was how it was with us. We were conscious of it very early on, and were very grateful to our mother for it. Home was simultaneously her and the house – the house around her and her inside the house. And she extended beyond herself with predictions of bad weather and years of disaster. She lived through two wars – nine years of it altogether – and she expected there to be a third. I think she expected it right up to her death, just as everyone else expects the next season. I think she only read the paper for that – to try to read between the lines whether war was getting closer. I don't remember her ever saying it was getting further away.

Sometimes, when we were children, she played at war to show us what it was like. She'd get hold of a stick about the same length as a gun, put it over her shoulder, and march up and down in front of us singing *Sambre et Meuse*. Then she'd burst into tears, and we'd try to console her. Yes, my mother liked the wars of men.

I believe that always, or almost always, in all childhoods and in all the lives that follow them, the mother represents madness. Our mothers always remain the strangest, craziest people we've ever met. Lots of people say, 'My mother was insane – I say it and I mean it. Insane.' People laugh a lot at the memory of their mothers. I suppose it is funny.

In the house in the country, at Neauphle-le-Château, I made a list of all the things that ought to be always in the house. There were a few dozen of them. We kept the list – it's still there – because it was I who'd written it down. It still includes everything.

Here at Trouville it's different – it's only an apartment. I wouldn't think of doing such a thing for here. But at Neauphle there have always been stocks of things. Here's the list:

table salt	butter	lavatory paper
pepper	tea	light bulbs
sugar	flour	kitchen soap
coffee	eggs	Scotchbrite
wine	tinned tomatoes	eau de Javel
potatoes	kitchen salt	washing powder
pasta	Nescafé	(hand)
rice	nuoc mam	Spontex
oil	bread	Ajax
vinegar	cheeses	steel wool
onions	yoghourt	coffee filters
garlic	window cleaner	fuses
milk		insulating tape

The list's still there, on the wall. We haven't added anything. We haven't taken to using any of the hundreds of new articles that have been invented in the twenty years since it was written.

Outer and inner order in a house. The outer order is the visible running of the house, and the inner order is that of the ideas, emotional phases and endless feelings connected with the children. A house as my mother conceived it was in fact *for* us. I don't think she'd have done it for a man or a lover. It's an activity that has nothing to do with men. They can build houses, but they can't make homes. As a general rule, men don't do anything for children. Nothing practical. They might take them to the cinema or out for a walk. But I think that's about all. The child is put into their arms when they get home from work – clean, changed, ready to go to bed. Happy. That makes a mountain of difference between men and women.

I seriously believe that to all intents and purposes the position of women hasn't changed. The woman is still responsible for everything in the house even if she has help, even if she's much more aware, much more intelligent, much bolder than before. Even if she has much more self-confidence. Even if she writes much more, a woman is just the same as she was before in relation to men. Her main ambition is still to watch over and look after the family. And even if she has changed socially, everything she does is done *on top of* that change. But have men changed? Almost not at all. Perhaps they don't shout so much. And they talk less. Yes. I can't see anything else. They can sometimes keep quiet. Be reduced to silence. Naturally. As a rest from the sound of their own voice.

The woman is the home. That's where she used to be, and that's where she is still. You might ask me, 'What if a man tries to be part of the home – will the woman let him?' I answer yes. Because then he becomes one of the children.

Men's needs have to be met just the same as children's. And women take the same pleasure in meeting them. Men think they're heroes – again just like children. Men love war, hunting, fishing, motorbikes, cars, just like children. When they're sleepy you can see it. And women like men to be like that. We mustn't fool ourselves. We like men to be innocent and cruel; we like hunters and warriors; we like children.

It's been going on for a long time. Ever since my son was a little boy *I*'ve brought the food from the kitchen and put it on the table. And when one course was finished and the next one was due, *I*'d go and fetch it without thinking, quite happily. Lots of women do it. Just like that, like me. They do it when the children are less than twelve years old, and they go on doing it afterwards. With the Italians, for example, you see women of eighty serving children of sixty. I've seen it myself in Sicily.

With a house – might as well admit it – it's rather as if you'd been given a boat, a yacht. And it's a very demanding job, running a house – the building itself and its human and other contents. It's only women who are not really quite women at all, frivolous women who have no idea, who neglect repairs. Now I've got where I wanted to get to – the repairs. I'd love to go into all the details, but perhaps the reader wouldn't understand why. Anyhow, here's what I have to say. Women who wait until there are three electric plugs that don't work, and the vacuum cleaner is unusable, and the taps drip, before they phone the plumber or buy some new plugs – these women have got it all wrong. As a rule it's women who've been neglected themselves who let things go like that – women who hope their husbands will notice and deduce that they're making their wives unhappy. Such women don't realize men never notice anything in a house run by their womenfolk: it's something they take for granted, something they got used to in their childhood with the woman who happened to be their mother. They can see very well that the plugs don't work, but what do they say? They say: 'Good heavens, the plugs don't work,' and go on with what they were doing. If the vacuum cleaner's broken they won't even notice. They simply don't see that sort of thing. Just like children – they don't notice anything. So women's behaviour is incomprehensible to men. If a woman omits to do something – forgets, or gets her own back by not buying new plugs – the men just won't take it in. Or they'll think she has reasons of her own for not buying new plugs or not getting the vacuum cleaner mended, and it would be tactless to ask what those reasons are. They're probably afraid they might suddenly be confronted by the women's despair, afraid they might be overwhelmed by despair themselves. People say men are 'adapting' now. It's hard to know what's really going on. Men try to 'adapt' themselves as regards practical things – one can accept that. But I don't really know what to think. I have a man friend who does the cooking and the housework. His wife doesn't do anything. She loathes housework, and doesn't know the first thing about cooking. And so my friend brings up the children and does the cooking; he washes the floors, does the shopping, makes the beds, sees to all the chores. And on top of all that he works to provide for them all. His wife wanted to be out of all the turmoil and have lovers whenever she felt like it. So she's taken a little house next door to the one her husband lives in with the two children, and he accepts this in order to keep her. Because she's the mother of his children. He accepts everything. He doesn't even suffer any more. What can you say to that? I personally feel slightly repelled by a man with such a strong sense of duty.

I'm told men often do the rough work and that you often see them in the household section of department stores. I don't even answer that sort of thing. Rough work is fun for men. To cut down trees after a day at the office isn't work – it's a kind of game. Of course, if you tell a man of ordinary build and average strength what needs doing, he does it. Wash up a couple of plates – he does it. Do the shopping – he does it. But he has a terrible tendency to think he's a hero if he goes out and buys some potatoes. Still, never mind.

People tell me I exaggerate. They say it all the time. Do you think exaggeration is the word? You talk of idealization, say I idealize women. Perhaps. Who's to say? Women could do with being idealized a bit.

You can think what you like about what I've just said. I must sound incomprehensible to you, talking about women's work. The main thing is to talk about them and their houses and their surroundings, and the way they manage other people's good.

Men and women are different, after all. Being a mother isn't the same as being a father. Motherhood means that a woman gives her body over to her child, her children; they're on her as they might be on a hill, in a garden; they devour her, hit her, sleep on her; and she lets herself be devoured, and sometimes she sleeps because they are on her body. Nothing like that happens with fathers.

But perhaps women secrete their own despair in the process of being mothers and wives. Perhaps, their whole lives long, they lose their rightful kingdom in the despair of every day. Perhaps their youthful aspirations, their strength, their love, all leak away through wounds given and received completely legally. Perhaps that's what it is – that women and martyrdom go together. And that women who are completely fulfilled by showing off their competence, their skill at games, their cooking and their virtue are two a penny.

Some women throw things away. I do it a lot.

For fifteen years I threw my manuscripts away as soon as the books came out. If I ask myself why, I think it was to wipe out the crime, to make it seem less important in my own eyes. It was so that I could 'pass' better in my own circle; to tone down the indecency of writing, if you were a woman, about forty years ago. I used to keep bits of sewing material and left-overs from the kitchen, but not manuscripts. So for all those years I burned them. And then one day someone said, 'Keep them for your son later on – you never know.'

The deed used to be done in the fireplace in the living room at Neauphle. It was total destruction. So did I know so early in my life that I was a writer? Probably. I can remember the days that followed the burnings. Everything became neat and virginal again. The house seemed lighter, the tables were free again – smooth and empty and without a trace.

In the past, women used to keep a lot of things. They kept children's toys, their homework, their first essays. They kept photographs from their own youth. Dark, blurred photographs that filled them with wonder. They kept the frocks they wore when they were girls, their wedding dresses, the orange blossom bouquets – but above all the photographs. Photographs of a world their children had never seen. Photographs with a meaning only for themselves.

One reason, perhaps the chief reason, why houses are flooded with material possessions is the longstanding ritual by which Paris is regularly submerged by sales, super-sales and final reductions. White sales, sales of left-overs from summer in the autumn and from autumn in the winter – women buy as some people take drugs, not because they need the things but because they're cheap. Then, when they get them home, as often as not they just throw them away. 'I don't know what came over me,' they say. As they might say if they spent a night in a hotel with a stranger.

In previous centuries most women would own two or three caracos or under-blouses, a camisole and a couple of petticoats. In the winter they used to wear them all, and in the summer they kept them tied up in a square of cotton. They took them along when they went away to work or to get married. Now women must own two hundred and fifty times as many clothes as they had a couple of centuries ago. But women's existence in the house has remained the same. A life that seems, even to the woman herself, to have been written down and described already. It's a sort of rôle in the usual sense of the word, but a part she seems to play to herself inevitably and almost unconsciously. And so women journey on through the theatre of profound loneliness that has constituted their lives for centuries. Their voyage hasn't been to the wars or the crusades; it's taken place in the house and in the forest and in their heads, riddled with beliefs and often crippled or ill. It was then that she was promoted to the rank of witch, like you, like me, and burned. But some summers, some winters, at certain times in certain centuries, what with the passage of time, the light, the noises, the wild animals ferreting about in the bushes and the cries of the birds, the women just took themselves off. Men haven't known about these departures. They can't know about that sort of thing. They're busy in one of the services or professions; they have a responsibility that preoccupies them all the time and prevents them from knowing anything about women or women's freedom. Very early on in history men lost their freedom. For a very long time the only men really close to women were the farm labourers, ill-used, helpless, often simple-minded, but cheerful. They stayed at home among the women and made them laugh, and the women hid them and saved them from death. At certain hours of the day, in those times, a solitary bird would cry out in the luminous dark before night fell. Even then night fell fast or slowly according to the day and the season or the state of the sky, or whether the pain in someone's heart was terrible or only slight.

The cottages in the forest had to be strong, to keep out both wolves and men. Let's suppose, for example, it's 1350. She's twenty, or thirty, or forty – not more. She seldom lives longer than that, yet. In the towns, plague is rampant. She's always hungry. Always afraid. But it's the loneliness around this scrawny figure, not the hunger and fear, that supports things as they are. Michelet can't bear to think about us, we're so thin and rickety. We produce ten children in order to keep one. Our husbands are far away.

When shall we tire of it, that forest of our despair? That Siam? And of man, who first set light to the pyre?

Forgive us for talking about it so often.

We're here. Where the story of our lives takes place. Nowhere else. We have no lovers but those in our sleep. We have no human desires. All we know is the faces of animals, the form and beauty of the forests. We're afraid of ourselves. Our bodies are cold. We are made up of cold and fear and desire. They used to burn us. They kill us still in Kuwait and the wilder parts of Arabia.

There are also houses that are too well made, too well thought out, completely without surprises, devised in advance by experts. By surprise I mean the unpredictable element produced by the way a house is used. Dining rooms are large because that's where guests are entertained, but kitchens are small – and getting smaller and smaller. Yet everyone squeezes in there to eat. When one person leaves the kitchen the others have to stand up to make way. But the habit persists.

Efforts are made to break it, but it's in the kitchen that everybody congregates at the end of the day. It's warm there, and you can be with Mother and hear her talk while she gets on with the cooking. Pantries and linen rooms don't exist any more either, yet they're really irreplaceable. Like big kitchens. And yards.

Nowadays you can't design your own house any more. It's frowned on. 'That was all very well in the past,' they tell you, 'but now there are experts and they can do it much better than you.'

This kind of attitude is increasingly common, and I dislike it intensely. In most modern houses there are none of the rooms you need to supplement the basics of kitchen and bedrooms. I mean rooms to keep things in. How can you do without them, and where are you supposed to do the ironing and the sewing and store things like nuts and apples and cheese and machines and tools and toys and so on?

And modern houses don't have passages, either, for children to play and run about in, and for dogs, umbrellas, coats and satchels. And don't forget that passages and corridors are where the young ones curl up and go to sleep when they're tired, and where you go and collect them to put them to bed. That's where they go when they're four years old and have had enough of the grown-ups and their philosophy. That's where, when they're unsure of themselves, they go and have a quiet cry.

Houses never have enough room for children, not even if they're castles. Children don't actually look at houses, but they know them and all their nooks and crannies better than their mothers do. They rummage about. They snoop around. They don't consciously look at houses any more than they look at the walls of flesh that enclose them before they can see anything at all – but they know them. It's when they leave the house that they look at it.

I'd like to talk about water, and cleanliness in houses. A dirty house is a terrible thing – the only people who can live in it are a dirty woman and a dirty husband and children. You can't live in it if you're not one of the dirty family. But a dirty house signifies something else to me, too – that the woman is in a dangerous state, a state of blindness. She's forgotten other people can see what she's done or left undone; and she's dirty herself without realizing it. Piles of washing up, grease everywhere, all the saucepans dirty. I've known people who waited until the dishes were crawling with maggots before they washed them up.

Some kitchens are frightening and fill one with despair. The worst of it is that children brought up amid dirt remain dirty for the rest of their lives. Dirty babies are the dirtiest things in the world.

In the colonies dirt was fatal. Dirt brought rats, and rats brought the plague. In the same way as piastres – piastre notes – brought leprosy.

So for me cleanliness is also a kind of superstition. Even now, when a person's mentioned to me I always ask if they're clean, just as I might ask if they're intelligent or sincere or honest.

I hesitated about keeping the passage on cleanliness in *The Lover* – I don't quite know why. As children, in the colonies, we were always in the water. We bathed in the rivers, we took showers morning and evening using water stored in jars, we went barefoot except in the street. But it was when the house was sluiced through with great buckets of water that the close fraternity between the children of the houseboys and the children of the Whites was celebrated. On those days my mother used to laugh with delight. I can't think of my childhood without thinking of water. The country where I was born is a land of water. The water of the lakes, the mountain torrents and the rice-fields. The muddy water of the rivers on the plain, in which people took shelter during storms. The rain came down so heavily it hurt. In ten minutes the garden was submerged. Who can ever describe the smell of the warm earth, steaming after a storm? Or of certain flowers. Of a jasmine in a garden. I'll never have been back to the country where I was born. Probably because the climate there, and Nature, seemed made for children. Once you're grown up it becomes external to you. You can't take such memories with you – you have to leave them where they came into being. I wasn't born anywhere.

Recently we had to break up the kitchen floor – here in France, at Neauphle – to put in an extra stair. The house is sinking. It's a very old place close to a pond: the soil's soft and very damp, and the house is gradually sinking. So the first tread on the stairs had become too high, too much effort. The mason had to dig a hole to get to the ballasting, then he found he couldn't get to the bottom of it. He dug deeper, and it still went on down further and further. But to what? What had the house been built on? He gave up digging and trying to find out. He filled in the hole. Cemented it over. And put in the new step.

CABOURG

It was at the end of the long promenade at Cabourg, near the harbour where the yachts are. There was a child on the beach flying a Chinese kite, as in *Summer 1980*. He didn't move from the spot where he was standing. All around him other children were playing football. I was quite a long way away, on the terrace. It was windy, and it would soon be dark. But the child didn't move, and his not moving became first irksome and then actually painful. Then by dint of peering hard at him, really concentrating, I saw what was the matter. Both his legs, which were as thin as sticks, were paralysed. Someone would no doubt be coming to take him home. Some of the other children were already leaving. He went on playing with the kite. Sometimes you say I'm going to kill myself, and then you go on with the book. Someone must have come and taken the child home before it got dark. The kite in the sky showed where he was. There couldn't be any mistake.

ANIMALS

I'd love to have lots of animals, lots of different ones. But you can't have a cow in Paris any more than you can go out of your mind. A cow tied up outside a block of flats in Paris means the lunatic asylum next morning for both the cow and its owner. Last week on television I saw a big she-bear come out from under the Arctic ice. She poked her head out and looked around. Then she hoisted herself out of her hole, and she was so weak she fell down. That big she-bear had had three cubs during the winter of 1986, and she hadn't moved or had anything to eat for three months. Her three cubs were very sturdy and well-nourished with her milk. But she herself was exhausted. She stayed out for one minute the first day, ten minutes the second day, and so on. After a week she rolled over and over down to the sea. As she swam about she watched the hole: the cubs weren't supposed to come out. But she didn't stay away long. She ate half a small seal and took the other half back to the cubs. She was as tall as General de Gaulle; she reminded me of him. Very lofty. A hundred yards away from her hole a male bear stood looking at her. She stopped in her tracks and looked back at him. He fled in terror.

TROUVILLE

The house at Trouville is where I live now. It's superseded
Neauphle and Paris. It was there I met Yann. He came into the
courtyard all lanky and thin. Walking very fast. He was going
through a depressive spell then. He was very pale. Scared at
first. Then it passed. I showed him the sea. It's a great luxury,
being able to see it from the balcony. When cities are bombed
there are always ruins and corpses left. But you can drop an
atomic bomb in the sea and ten minutes later it's back as it was
before. You can't change the shape of water. While I'm writing
that Yann came to my house in 1980, he's speaking on the
telephone. He spends ten hours a day doing that – he's going
through a telephonic spell now. The bill came to four thousand
five hundred and fifty francs for the month of August. He
phones up people he doesn't know. And people he's met only
once in his life. And people in Austria or Germany or Italy that
he hasn't seen for ten years. Every time he calls someone up he
howls with laughter. It makes it very difficult to work. Afterwards he goes out for walks in the hills. Sometimes he'll phone
someone three days running and then give up on them
altogether. Often because of something they've said. Such as:
'Where would I be without my wife?' The humble remark of
all the great men of this century, from Dumézil to de Gaulle.

THE STAR

Death, the fact of death coming towards you, is also a memory. Like the present. It's completely here, like the memory of what has already happened and the thought of what is still to come. Like the accumulated springs of years gone by, and like the spring that's coming now, a leaf at a time, on the brink of being here. And death is like the explosion of a star, which occurred seventy-four million years ago and yet is visible from the earth one night in February 1987. A time as precise as the moment when a leaf bursts forth. Death is that present too. And the thought that you might never have known about it.

THE M.D. UNIFORM

Madeleine Renaud is dressed by Yves Saint-Laurent: he makes her some dresses, someone puts them on her, and lo and behold she goes about in them. You wonder if she knows that the dress she's wearing is new. These days Madeleine doesn't know so much as she used to. But we're very fond of one another, and I think she still knows that. I often think she and I are the only two women who don't care about the clothes we wear. But it's more complicated than that. For fifteen years I've had a uniform – the M.D. uniform. It apparently created a 'Duras look', which was taken over by a fashion designer last year: black cardigan, straight skirt, polo-neck sweater and short boots in winter. I said I didn't care about clothes, but that's wrong. A uniform is an attempt to reconcile form and content, to match what you think you look like with what you'd like to look like, what you think you are with what you want to suggest. You find this match without really looking for it. And once it's found it's permanent. And eventually it comes to define you. This is what's happened to me, and it's a help. I'm very short. This has meant I've never been able to wear most of the clothes the majority of women wear. My whole life has been affected by this difficulty, and the need to avoid wearing anything that might call attention to my size. The solution was to stop people thinking about it by always wearing the same clothes. So that people would notice the sameness of the uniform rather than the reason why it was adopted. I don't carry a handbag any more, either. It's changed my life. But even before I started wearing a cardigan, it was already a kind of different sameness.

I didn't need to dress up, because I was a writer. And the argument applies even before you start writing. Men like women who write. Even though they don't say so. A writer is a foreign country.

So now you know everything.

WRITERS' BODIES

Writers' bodies are involved in their writing. Writers invite sexuality. Like kings and other people in power. As regards men, it's as if they'd slept with our minds, penetrated our minds at the same time as our bodies. There haven't been any exceptions as far as I'm concerned. The same kind of fascination operated even with lovers who weren't intellectuals. And for a worker a woman who writes books – that's something he'll never have. It's like that all over the world, for all writers, men and women alike. They're sex objects *par excellence*. When I was still very young I was attracted to elderly men because they were writers. I've never been able to imagine sex without intelligence, or intelligence without a kind of absence from oneself. Lots of intellectuals are clumsy lovers – unadventurous, apprehensive and absent-minded. It was all the same to me as long as when they weren't with me they were, as writers, just as absent about their own bodies. I've noticed that writers who are superb at making love are much more rarely great writers than those who are scared and not so good at it. Talent and genius evoke rape, just as they evoke death. Sham writers don't have these problems. They're sound and healthy and you can go with them quite safely. When both members of a couple are writers the wife says: 'My husband's a writer.' The husband says: 'My wife writes too.' The children say: 'My father writes books, and so does my mother, sometimes.'

ALAIN VEINSTEIN

This is a bad period for me. It's the end of a book, and there's a kind of loneliness, as if the closed book were going on still somewhere else, inside me. And that again I can't get hold of it properly. I can't talk about it. Throughout the whole broadcast with Alain Veinstein last night (25 November, on France Culture – it lasted two hours), I couldn't utter a sentence. It was as if I'd been struck speechless. It was very strange. Veinstein would just wait, and I always managed to say something in the end. Then I'd stop again. I wondered what had happened to me, what sort of nightmare had struck me. I don't really know what the answer is. Of course, there was that affair. The affair that started when I was sixty-five, with Y.A., who's a homosexual. That's probably the most unexpected thing that's happened to me in the latter part of my life – the most terrifying and the most important. It's like what happens in *The War*. But in this case the man is here, I'm not waiting for him, he isn't in the camps, he's here, guarding me against death. That's what he's doing, though he tries to ignore it. He thinks he doesn't know. But one thing's clear, and that's that neither he nor I can bear the idea of going on living after the other one dies. We know we love one another. But we don't say anything. It's unapproachable, even by us. There wasn't only the affair, there was also the backbreaking book, and Yann blocking its way, like a lunatic, throwing himself on it as if to stop it from being written, and only making sure that it was.

In the American Hospital, while I was in a coma, I had lucid intervals in which I saw he was with me. These moments were very rare and very brief, but I could see he desired me. I asked him about it. I said, 'When I was in a coma and you didn't know whether I was going to survive, you desired me.' He said: 'Yes, I did.' We spoke, but came to no conclusion. I couldn't speak any more, or write. I couldn't even hold a spoon – I dribbled and spilt things everywhere. I'd forgotten how to walk. I got mixed up. I fell down. And that was the woman Y.A. desired and loved.

RACINE'S FORESTS

When I'm at Trouville I can't imagine going back to Paris. I can't think what I'd do there now. I see very few people these days. But it's much worse than that. Much worse. I *can't* live in Paris any more. You get yourself into that sort of situation, without thinking, and there you are. I can't see even a couple of days ahead in my life. Either with this man or without him – it's the same as in quite different affairs from ours. It's true – to confirm what I said to Veinstein – it's not a question of suffering. It's a ratification of an original despair, dating you might almost say from childhood, as if all of a sudden you experienced the same sense of impossibility as you felt when you were eight years old. A sense of impossibility when you looked at things, people, the sea, life, the limited nature of your own body; or the trees in the forest, which you couldn't get to without risking death; or the sailing of liners, which seemed to be going away for ever and ever; or my mother, mourning my dead father with a grief we knew to be childish but which might take her away from us. That must be the great thing about old age. I haven't reached it yet, but I'm getting closer. That's the obvious thing people get wrong when they don't establish their own personal way of behaving. My mother always cried in the appropriate situations, and she always laughed as one's supposed to do, after a dinner party, at the coarse jokes made by the men. Sometimes we used to feel it so terribly when she acted just like everyone else that when she came home we almost had to forgive her. We were very distant. When she came home from parties where she'd pretended to be amused, we knew she hadn't been amused at all, she'd nearly died of boredom. She did all the right things to be like other people, but it never worked with us. We knew she'd been somewhere else, unknowingly, in some sacred state outside which we couldn't bear to see her. There was something sacred about her, and we were the only ones who knew it. If anyone knows there's something sacred about Van Gogh, and Matisse, Nicolas de Staël and Monet, it's because they've had that sort of childhood, spent in the same kind of unwearying scrutiny of unfathomable depth that we directed upon our mother. I want to bring Van Gogh and the rest into the business with Yann because it too has something sacred about it. Music is sacred too. I've found you have to look a long while for the sacred in writing: but the wind of the sacred does blow through the great forests of Racine. Through the tops of the trees in the great Racinian forest. That's Racine. Not in detail, not as he's read and thought about. It's his music. It's music speaking. Yes, that's what it is, though people often get it wrong. That's Mozart, and Racine. It shouts at you.

THE TRAIN FROM BORDEAUX

I was sixteen years old. I still looked like a child. It was when we'd come back from Saigon, after the Chinese lover. It was on a night train, the train from Bordeaux, in about 1930. I was with my family – my two brothers and my mother. We were in a third-class compartment with eight seats in it, and I think there were two or three other people besides us. There was also a young man sitting opposite me and looking at me. He must have been about thirty. It must have been in the summer. I was still wearing the sort of light-coloured dress I used to wear in the colonies, with sandals and no stockings. The man asked me about my family, and I told him about what it was like living in the colonies: the rains, the heat, the veranda, how different it was from France, the walks in the forest, and the *baccalauréat* exam I was going to take that year. That sort of thing – the usual kind of conversation you have in a train when you pour out your own and your family's life history. And then all of a sudden we noticed everyone else was asleep. My mother and brothers had dropped off soon after we left Bordeaux. I spoke quietly so as not to wake them. If they'd heard me telling someone else all our business their yells and threats would soon have put a stop to it. And our whispered conversation had sent the other three or four passengers to sleep too. So the man and I were the only two still awake. And that was how it started, suddenly, at exactly the same moment, and with a single look. In those days people didn't speak about such things, especially in circumstances like that. All at once we couldn't go on talking. We couldn't go on looking at one another either; we felt weak, shattered. I was the one who said we ought to get some sleep so as not to be too tired when we got to Paris in the morning. He was sitting near the door so he switched out the light. There was an empty seat between us. I curled up on it and closed my eyes. I heard him open the door. He went out and came back with a blanket and spread it over me. I opened my eyes to smile and say thank you. He said: 'They turn off the heating at night and it gets cold towards morning.' I went to sleep. I was wakened by his warm soft hand on my legs; very slowly it straightened them out and tried to move up towards my body. I opened my eyes just a fraction. I could see he was looking at the other people in the carriage, watching them; he was afraid. I very slowly moved my body towards him and put my feet against him. I gave them to him. He took them. With my eyes shut, I followed all his movements. They were slow even at first, then more and more slow and controlled until the final paroxysm of pleasure, as upsetting as if he'd cried out.

For a long while there was nothing except the noise of the train. It was going faster and the noise was deafening. Then it became bearable again. He put his hand on me. Distraught, still warm, afraid. I held it in mine for a moment, then let it go, let it do as it liked.

The noise of the train came back again. The hand went away, stayed away for some time. I don't remember how long – I must have drowsed off.

Then it came back.

It stroked me all over first, then my breasts, stomach and hips, in a kind of overall gentleness disturbed every so often by new stirrings of desire. Sometimes it would stop. It halted over my sex, trembling, about to take the bait, burning hot again. Then it moved on. Finally it resigned itself, quietened down, became kind in order to bid the child goodbye. All around the hand was the noise of the train. All around the train, the darkness. The silence of the corridors within the noise of the train. The stops, waking people up. He got off into the darkness. When I opened my eyes in Paris his seat was empty.

THE BOOK

The book is about two people who love one another. But who love one another unawares. It happens outside the book. What I'm saying now is something I didn't want to say in the book but which I mustn't forget to say now, even though it's hard to find the words. The essence of this love is that it can't be written. It's a love that writing hasn't yet reached. It's too strong, stronger than the people themselves. It's not at all organized. It happens at night, mostly while they're asleep. Loves are usually organized to start with, even if only around a central inhibition. A love creates habits and customs for itself. The people eat, sleep, lay one another, quarrel, make up, attempt suicide, are fond of one another sometimes. Sometimes they part and come back together again. Sometimes they talk about other things – they don't weep all the time. But in this case they don't do anything. They don't make love, they just wait in the dark; sometimes he wants to kill her. Personally I think he ought to have killed her, he was bound to have felt like it, but it struck me as rather a forced and premature solution. I'm tempted to say it's an absurd love, without real subjects, like the smile without a face in *Alice*; but that would be abstract and wrong. No, I come back to what I was saying, that it's a love that loves even now, which invades everything, and which is immune from anything anyone may say about it, for reasons that might be called religious. For it resembles a need to suffer, an obscure need to suffer in order to recall an absence without an image, without a face, without a voice. But which, like music, sweeps the whole body towards the emotion that goes with deliverance from some formal burden.

Yes, the book is about an unavowed love between people prevented by an unknown force from saying they love one another. And who do love one another. It's not clear. It can't be stated. It's elusive, helpless. And yet it exists. In a confusion which they share, which is peculiar to them, and which arises from the similarity of their feelings. Are they conscious of any of what passes between them and binds them together? I don't know. They know more than other people do about the silence that should be kept about love; but they don't know how to deal with the experience. Instead, they have another affair, as if they were different people. When one says people love one another one usually means they love each other with physical passion. These are people who don't know how to love one another and yet do have a love affair. But the word to express it never crosses their lips, nor does desire come to their sex, to express it and vent it and then be able to chat and have a drink. Nothing but tears.

I know the people in the book, but I don't know their story, just as I don't know my own. I have no story, just as I have no life. My story is pulverized every day, every second of every day, by the immediacy of life, and it's impossible for me to see clearly what's usually called one's life. Only the thought of death puts me back together again, and the love of this man and of my child. I've always lived as if it were impossible for me to resemble any model existence, any given pattern. I wonder in what terms other people tell their life histories. Accounts based on chronology or external facts seemed to be the most popular. You start at the beginning of your life, then trundle along towards the present on the rails of public events, wars, changes of address, marriages, etc.

Some books are perfect as they stand: *Summer 1980, The Atlantic Man*, the Vice-Consul crying out in the Shalimar Gardens, the beggar woman, the smell of leprosy, *M.D., Lol V. Stein, The Lover, The War, The War, The War* and *The Lover*, Hélène Lagonelle, the dormitories, the light from the river. *The Sea Wall* became perfect in that sense too: the camouflage, the replacement of some personal elements by others less apt to pique the reader's curiosity and thus less likely to distract him from the story I wanted him to read – everything was integrated into the original story, which itself disappeared. This went on right up to *The Lover*. So there are, in my life, two little girls and me. The one in *The Sea Wall*. The one in *The Lover*. And the one in the family photographs. I can't see what happened while I was writing this last book, during the terrible summer of 1986. In that story, which actually happened although it is transposed, it's difficult to find the untruth, the point where the book lies, and on what level, in which adverb. It may lie in just one word. I don't think it lies about desire. It must always happen like that when the man is repelled by your body. And yet the book does tell a story that actually happened. I've just made a special and not a general case of it. Perhaps the time for writing it had gone by; I had to remember having suffered. The suffering was still there, but it was more even. The same with the emotion. In *The Lover* and *The War* the emotion is still warm and pulsating. It echoes through the slightest breath in those two books; I can hear the voices too. But here, no; I can't see or hear anything. I've merged into the characters, and what I'm doing is telling of an impossible (just as I'd tell of a possible) affair between a woman and a homosexual, whereas what I really want to tell of is a love affair which is always possible even though it seems impossible to people unfamiliar with writing. For writing isn't supposed to concern itself with that kind of possibility or impossibility. It may be that I was trying, unsuccessfully, to say the same thing as I'm saying now – i.e., it wasn't a love affair that took place between the characters: it was just love. Perhaps what I wanted to say was that once, one night, in the confines of their relationship, love appeared like a shaft of light in the darkness. That once, at a certain moment, the affair became love.

If it upsets me so much to write untruthfully, even slightly, it must be because it doesn't often happen. But I'm probably still too much affected by writing the book to know. I must get to feel better disposed towards it again; I need to stop treating it as some hostile and dangerous object, a weapon directed against myself. What happened? It's as if I were being told that not everything comes within the reach of writing; that whether you like it or not, writing stops short at closed doors. Whereas I believe the opposite – that it gets through everything, doors that are closed included, no matter why they're closed. But there's a sort of latent didacticism *à la* Barthes in the book: I have ideas, and I display them, so that the novel is sometimes *explained* like the sort that wins prizes. In other words I didn't bring it off. I put the sea and a river in the middle of the story, but that wasn't enough to untame the characters and their love. I was too involved. It remained too far away.

I don't know what I ought to have done. What took place every day was not what happened every day. Sometimes what didn't take place was the most important thing that happened. It was when nothing took place that it was most interesting. I ought to have entered into the book myself, with all my paraphernalia – my ravaged face, my age, my profession, my roughness, my insanity; and you ought to have stayed in the book too, with all your paraphernalia – your smooth face, your age, your idleness, your terrible roughness, your insanity, and your fabulous angelicness. And even that wouldn't have been enough.

We snapped our fingers at all compromises, all the usual 'arrangements'. We confronted the impossibility of that love without flinching or trying to escape. It was a mysterious love, impossible to imagine. It was so strange we used to laugh at it. We couldn't recognize it, and we took it as it came – impossible – without doing anything to suffer less, without running away, not trying to kill it, not going away. And it wasn't enough.

All the time before I gave in the manuscript, right up to the last minute, I thought I might still avoid handing it over to be printed. But I was the only one to think that, and it was too late, and in the end they were right to publish it.

QUILLEBEUF

I told you Quillebeuf triggered off the desire to write. In fact it was the other way round. It was because I already wanted to write that the Quillebeuf story stuck in my mind as it did. But I'm talking to you from the outside about a book that isn't yet written. Let me explain: the book that grew in my mind out of Quillebeuf was supposed to come before a third book, the one I've just finished. And I'd have been writing the Quillebeuf book now if I hadn't lost the manuscript. But I had to make another trip to Trouville to look for it.

Time went by.

The ten lost pages were found among the drafts of the book that's already been published.

The new book was finished in March 1987 and delivered to the publisher six months after *Blue Eyes*.

It's a long time since I've liked a book as much as I like that one.

THE MAN WHO WAS A LIE

I recently tried to write a book that was going to be called *The Man Who Was a Lie*. It was about a man who lied. He lied all the time, to everyone and about everything that had ever happened to him. Deception crossed his lips even before the words to express it. He didn't feel himself doing it. He didn't lie about Baudelaire or Joyce, or blow his own trumpet or boast about his amorous adventures. Nothing like that. He lied about the price of a pullover, or a journey he'd made on the métro. Or about the time a film began at the cinema, a meeting with a friend, a conversation, a menu, all the details of a trip he'd been on, including the names of the towns he'd visited. About his family, his mother, his nephews. It was completely uninteresting. At first it was maddening too. But after a month or two you got used to it.

He was a marvellously talented writer. Very shrewd, very funny, very very charming. He was also an extraordinarily gifted talker. Born into the middle class, but courteous as a prince. He'd been brought up like a king by his mother, but that never affected his naturalness or his charm.

If I make him out to be so irresistible it's because he was a born lover, a born lover of women. At a glance he could see them, make out the very essence of their desire. And be overwhelmed by it in a way I've never seen in anyone else. It's that aspect of him I want to talk about – the gift he had for taking women into himself and loving them even before he'd experienced their beauty or the sound of their voice.

Women were the main concern of his life, and many of them knew it as soon as they saw him; as soon as they saw the look in his eyes. He had only to look at a woman and he was her lover.

He was a violent lover, with a roughness at once controlled and wild, at once terrifying and polite.

I've tried several times to write about him, but at every attempt his deceitfulness hid everything from me, including his face and his eyes. Now, suddenly, for the first time, I can do it.

He rented an apartment just for himself. He went there to escape the scrutiny of friends and family alike. He saw himself as young and eternally attractive; he wanted to live like a young man, lunching off a snack, dining in a restaurant, and having all the women at his disposal – Frenchwomen in the winter and English girls in the spring. In the summer he went to Saint-Tropez. He used to follow women around. That's how it was in 1950. He'd made up his mind to follow his passion for women through, even if it meant suffering and danger, and no matter how old he lived to be. He wanted to be overwhelmed by them, not to let any of his subjection go to waste. To turn his desire into something creative. Even if he'd seduced them only once, through a glance in the street, the essence of his sex never forgot them. Once obsessed by

desire for a woman he'd set his heart on, he lived only for
that passion. Other women ceased to exist. These periods of
love for one woman had the intensity of a religious devotion.
He never planned anything in such cases. He could neither
plan his desire for a woman nor decide to behave carefully
and with moderation in the matter. All he could do was die
of wanting her.

He was a magnificent and excellent fellow in every way,
but worn out with always expiring without ever actually
dying of it, and hoping for death as much as for passion. His
only knowledge of himself came via women. They plunged
him into a tragic and irresistible emotion. I've seen him, at
night, in bars, go suddenly pale at the sight of certain women
and look as if he were about to faint. While he was looking
at one of them he completely forgot all the others. Each
seemed to him the last and only one. And that went on until
he died.

Death struck first one spring day at Etretat. But he didn't
die of that – the awful inability to have anything to do with
a woman for two years. Not allowed to smoke. Not allowed
to love. Not allowed to make love. His life did go on, however,
like that. But it had been a very bad coronary, and he died of
it ten years later.

It was during those two years that he went on with a book
he'd started some years before. A man's book. Very long;
about the fifties. He won the biggest of the French prizes, the
Médicis, with it. That made him happy.

Once – I think not long before he died – he told a friend
we had in common that once in his life he'd loved a woman
on a long-term basis. That for several years he wasn't un-
faithful to her. But without having planned it. Why? He

didn't know. Once in his life he'd managed to achieve a love that was exclusive and lasting. Why he'd reached that degree of intensity with her rather than another, he didn't know. He thought it was probably because of her rather than himself. That it must always be like that. It was always the woman, the woman's desire, that kept lovers together. Love, the course taken by an affair, everything, depended on the permanence of the woman's desire. When the woman's desire ended, so did the man's – or, if it didn't, he became wretched, humiliated, mortally wounded, lonely.

He thought men and women were as fundamentally different in their flesh, their desire and their shape as if they belonged to two different orders of creation.

He died in a one-night hotel room. The hotel is very close to where I live. I've been told she was very young and beautiful, with auburn hair and green eyes like the woman in his novel. She was newly married and until that evening had always refused him.

She had to wait for him. He was late. He took his time and smoked a cigarette. He'd started smoking again a year before. He wanted her very much. For months he'd been asking her to go with him just once to a hotel. Finally she gave in. He was very pale. Unable to conceal his emotion. Since his coronary he was afraid every time he made love to a woman. His death took only a second. A sudden death. He didn't have time to see it coming. She told about it. Suddenly she knew he was dead by the weight of his body – he was already inside her. She realized instantly. She rushed out of the hotel, telling the reception desk as she went by that someone was dead in such and such a room and they'd better call the police.

My memory of him is very clear: he's striding along the street, very well-dressed. I can still see the colours: English shoes with metal tips on the soles, loose mustard-coloured pullover, light-brown corduroy trousers. He has very long legs and a graceful and remarkably even walk; instead of holding him back, his body is so slight it impels him forward. He looks about him as he walks along. His eyes have the blankness of someone half-asleep, and yet he looks about him. If anyone speaks his name it's the same: he looks around and hides behind his own gaze. He's watching out for women in Chanel suits, bored by winter afternoons.

One day a very young woman asked if I would see her and talk about him. Not the one in the hotel. His death had been a tragedy for her, and she still hadn't quite got over it. She was looking for someone who could talk adequately about him, about all that intelligence, profundity and purity. I said almost nothing.

We'd met at a party one evening at Christmas. I'd gone there on my own to find a lover. We left together, but I changed my mind and insisted on going home. We had a friend in common – everyone knew everyone else in Paris then, just as they do now – and he phoned this friend – the same one as before – and asked him to tell me he'd be waiting for me in a certain café. For five or six hours every day he sat and waited for me in that café, looking out at the street – every day for a week. But I held out. I went out every day, but not in that direction. And all the time I was dying for a new love affair. On the eighth day I went into the café as if I were mounting to the scaffold.

PHOTOGRAPHS

It's when people move that photos get lost. My mother moved between twenty and twenty-five times in the course of her life, and that's how our family photos got lost. They fall down and get stuck behind drawers, and if you're lucky you find them the next time you move. After a hundred years they're as brittle as glass. Have I told you this before? One day, in the fifties, underneath the drawer of a wardrobe that we'd bought in Indochina, I found a postcard dated 1905 and addressed to someone then living in the rue Saint-Benôit, where I live now. Photographs – one can't live without them – already existed when I was young. For my mother, a photograph of a young child was sacred. To see a child again as it used to be when it was young, you looked at a photograph. People still do. It's very mysterious. The only photos of Yann that I like are the ones taken ten years ago, before I knew him. They have in them what I look for in him now – the innocence of not knowing anything yet, not knowing what would happen to us in September 1980, for better or worse.

In the late nineteenth century people used to go and have their photographs taken by the village photographer in order to exist more convincingly, like the people of Vinh Long in *The Lover*.

PHOTOGRAPHS

There aren't any photographs of one's great-grandmother. You can search the whole world over and you won't find any. When you think of it, the absence of photographs leaves a serious gap; it even presents a problem. How did they live without photos? There's nothing left of anyone's face or body after they die. No record of their smile. And if you'd told people there'd be such a thing as photography one day, they'd have been shattered and appalled. But contrary to what they'd have thought and to what people still think today, I believe photographs promote forgetting. That's how it tends to work now. The fixed, flat, easily available countenance of a dead person or an infant in a photograph is only one image as against the million other images that exist in the mind. And the sequence made up by the million images I will never alter. It's a confirmation of death. I don't know what use photography was put to in its early days, in the first half of the nineteenth century. I don't know what it meant to the individual in the midst of his solitude – whether he valued it because it enabled him to see the dead again or because it allowed him to see himself. The second, I'm sure. One's always embarrassed or delighted by one's own photograph, but in either case also surprised. You're always more unreal to yourself than other people are. In life, even if you include the false perspective of the mirror, you're the person you see the least; and the best, composite image of yourself, the one you want to keep, is the specially prepared face that you try to summon up when you pose for your photograph.

THE CUTTER-OFF OF WATER

It happened on a summer's day in a village in eastern France, perhaps three or four years ago, in the afternoon. A man from the water board came to cut off the water in the house of some people who were slightly special, slightly different from most. Backward, you might say. The local authorities let them live in a disused railway station. The high-speed train now ran through that part of the country. The man did odd jobs in the village. And they must have had some help from the town hall. They had two children, one four years old and the other a year and a half.

The high-speed train ran close by where they lived. They were very poor, and couldn't pay their gas and electricity or water bills. And one day a man came to cut the water off. He saw the woman, who didn't say anything. The husband wasn't there. Just the rather backward wife, the child of four and the baby of eighteen months. The man looked just like other men. I named him the Cutter-off of Water. He realized it was the middle of summer. He knew, because he was experiencing it too, that it was a very hot summer. He saw the eighteen-month-old baby. But he'd been told to cut off the water, so that's what he did. He did his job and cut the water off. And left the woman without any water to bathe the children; without any water to give them to drink.

That evening the woman and her husband took the two children and went and lay down on the rails of the high-speed train that ran past the disused station. They all died together. Just a hundred yards to go. Lie down. Keep the children quiet. Sing them to sleep perhaps.

People say the train stopped.

Well, that's the story.

The man from the water board said he went and cut off the water. He didn't say he'd seen the child, that the child was there with its mother. He said she didn't argue, didn't ask him not to cut the water off.

That's what we know.

I take the story I've just told and all of a sudden I hear my own voice. She didn't do anything, she didn't argue. That's how it was. We find out through the man from the water board. There was no reason why he shouldn't do what he did, because she didn't ask him not to. Is that what we're supposed to understand? The whole thing is enough to drive you mad.

So I go on. I try to see. She didn't tell the man about the two children because he could see them; she didn't say anything about the hot summer because he was there in it. She let the Cutter-off of Water go. She stayed there alone with the children for a moment, then she went into the village. She went into a café she knew. We don't know what she said to the woman who owned it. I don't know what she said. I don't know if the owner of the café said anything. What we do know is that the woman didn't say anything about death. She might have told the other woman what had happened, but she didn't say she meant to kill herself, to kill her two children and her husband and herself.

As the reporters didn't know what she'd said to the owner of the café they didn't mention the incident. By incident I mean what happened when she went out with the two children after she'd decided the whole family must die. When she went off for some reason we don't know, to do or say something she had to do or say before she died.

Now I restore the silence in the story between the time the water was cut off and the time when she got back from the café. In other words, I restore the profound silence of literature. That's what helps me forward, helps me get inside the story. Without it I'd have to remain outside. She could just have waited for her husband and told him she'd decided they must die. But instead she went into the village and into the café.

If she had explained herself she wouldn't have interested me. I'm passionately interested in Christine Villemin because she can't put two sentences together; because like the other woman she is full of unfathomable violence. There's an instinctive behaviour in their two cases that one can try to explore, that one can give back to silence. It's much more difficult, much less appropriate, to give men's behaviour back to silence because silence isn't a masculine thing. From the most ancient times, silence has been the attribute of women. So literature is women too. Whether it speaks of them or they actually write it, it's them.

And so that woman, who people thought wouldn't have spoken because she never did – she must have spoken. Not of her decision. No. She must have said something that took the place of her decision; something that was equivalent to it for her and that would be equivalent to it for all the people who heard the story. Perhaps it was something about the heat. The words ought to be held sacred.

It's at times like this that language attains its ultimate power. Whatever she said to the owner of the café, her words said everything. Those three words, the last before the implementation of death, were the equivalent of those people's silence all their lives. But no one has remembered what those words were.

In life that happens all the time, when someone goes away, or dies, or when there's a suicide no one ever anticipated. People forget what was said, what went before and should have warned them.

All four of them went and lay down on the rails of the high-speed train near the station. The man and the woman held a child each in their arms, and waited for the train. The Cutter-off of Water didn't have an enemy in the world.

I add to the story of the Cutter-off of Water the fact that the woman, who everyone said was retarded, knew something for certain anyhow: she knew she couldn't count, now any more than ever, on anyone's helping her and her family out. She knew she was abandoned by everyone, by the whole of society, and that the only thing left for her to do was die. She knew that. It's a terrible, fundamental, awful knowledge. So the question of her backwardness ought to be reconsidered, if anyone ever talked about her again. Which they won't.

This is probably the last time she'll ever be remembered. I was going to mention her name, but I don't know what it was.

The case has been closed.

What stays in the mind is a child's unslaked thirst in a sweltering summer a few hours before it died, and a young retarded mother wandering about until it was time.

FIGON, GEORGES

My friend Georges Figon was thirty-five when he was granted
a remission. Between the ages of eighteen and thirty-five he'd
spent fourteen years and seven months in prison. There's
something I shall never accept about his story: its end, his
death. I'm talking about it here in order to put it on record.
Figon was happy for a few weeks after he was let out. Then
suddenly it all went wrong. One day depression descended
upon him, and wherever he went after that he could never
throw it off. Nothing would help. And it lasted right up to
his death. For that's what he died of, that's why he got killed
by the police. Figon died of despair, because he realized that
the story of his imprisonment was useless outside jail –
it couldn't be told to people who'd never been to prison
themselves. He realized that together with all the other things
prison meant, it meant above all this dispossession. Once
he'd left Fresnes he descended into solitude once and for all.
We listened to him for hours, days, nights. But as soon as
our emotion wore off, the story that obsessed Figon himself
began to seem more distant to us, and he knew it. Why?
Probably because the person who has experienced the thing
he tells about and the person who listens to it need to have
some ordinary things in common – work, profession, morals,

political persuasion and so on. If Figon had written a book, it ought to have been for inmates of the prisons he'd been in. Between prison and freedom however relative there is nothing in common, not the remotest similarity. Even reading and sleeping are different. If Figon was ever happy it was in prison, when he was acting as librarian and hatching a book about prison in the same way as he might have plotted a robbery. He thought his book would change society. But he didn't bring it off, and that killed him. He died because he couldn't convey what he knew about prison to anyone else. He described day-to-day life inside with astonishing accuracy. He knew the staff of all the prisons he'd been in individually, and the CVs of all the lawyers from examining magistrate to public prosecutor. But it didn't do him any good. Probably part of the trouble was his own purity, his desire to reproduce faithfully what had happened. He got bogged down in verisimilitude, lost in the swamp of fact. If he'd forgotten everything and then reinvented it, above all if he'd depersonalized his experience, he might not have died in despair. He ought to have cheated, recast for others what he had undergone himself. His life out of prison consisted of going over and over his life in prison. He was afraid of forgetting. No doubt imprisonment is a kind of initiation completely different from any ordeal we 'respectable' people encounter. I can remember some of the details. Even the most trivial request would only be granted after bawling and threatening and a good deal of waiting. This was all thirty years ago, and there was no television or radio in prisons then. I think cigarettes were the only thing you could barter.

I've re-read the above. When I say Figon was never as happy as when he was in prison, I ought to add that I'm speaking of the happiness he got from looking forward to the happiness he'd enjoy when he was free. The only freedom he knew was inside the prison at Fresnes, and without prison around him to help him savour the happiness of freedom, the happiness vanished. It's probably always like that.

WALESA'S WIFE

I see journalists as the manual workers, the labourers of the word. Journalism can only be literature when it is passionate. Cournot's articles have become part of a marvellous book on the theatre. And sometimes in a paper you suddenly come across a real text, especially in the law reports and the odd news items. And Serge Daney, especially perhaps on tennis, is in the process of becoming a writer. Serge July's a writer too, especially when he writes fast. And André Fontaine.

Godard once went on 'Seven out of Seven' on TV and said what he thought of television journalists. It was after Walesa won the Nobel Prize. His wife went to receive the prize for him because the Polish government wouldn't let him go to Stockholm himself. And Godard said to the journalists: 'When Walesa's wife went up to receive the prize she was centre of attention, and for the first time for ages, quite unexpectedly, you had a chance to shoot pictures of a beautiful woman. But you didn't attempt to get her in close-up. Why not? You don't even know. I think it may have been just because she *was* beautiful.' And he added: 'And because she wasn't a model or an actress, whose profession it is to be seen.'

Godard said something that needed saying.

It was marvellous, the idea of that young Polish woman going to get the prize in her husband's stead. But in actual fact it was deathly boring. Throughout the whole ceremony you waited to see her up close, and you never did. It was very strange. As if certain shots and angles weren't allowed. As if the TV coverage was doomed to failure because it could only convey the principle of Walesa's wife's presence and not actually show her beauty.

A real news programme would have shown her because she was more than Walesa himself – she was the woman he loved. That day she was the map that enabled you to find the way to the whole, to the entirety to which she was linked. Just as a forest is linked to someone passing through it on the way to their death. Or like someone's dress, or hair, or a letter, or a footprint in a cave, or a voice on the telephone. A real news item is both physical and subjective. An image shown, written or spoken. But always indirect.

Sometimes I think polemical journalism, reviled as it is, is the best. At least it reinstates ignorance and makes people doubt what they're being asked to believe. You read it in order to correct it. You can adapt it to your own purposes. It's sad, all the trouble they went to, to make a mess of Stockholm and the little Polish pony, Walesa's wife.

THE TELLY AND DEATH

It started when Michel Foucault died. The day after his death there was a piece about him on television, showing him giving a lecture at the Collège de France. Practically all you could hear was a sort of crackling in the background. His voice was there, but drowned by the voice of the commentator saying this was the voice of Michel Foucault delivering one of his lectures at the Collège de France. Soon after that Orson Welles died, and the same thing happened. You heard a very clear voice saying that the very faint and inaudible voice you could scarcely hear at all was that of Orson Welles, who had just died. It's come to be the rule whenever anyone well known dies – the aural image of the deceased is swamped by that of the journalist telling you that what you're listening to is of course the voice of so-and-so who's just passed on. Some editor no doubt discovered that if the presenter and the deceased both spoke at once it would save a minute's transmission time, and they could go on all the sooner to sport or some other more interesting and amusing subject.

In France we have no way of getting in touch with television journalists and telling them they shouldn't switch too fast from the mournful smile they wear to talk about the hostages to the grin they use for the weather forecast. It won't do. There are other ways. For instance they might just pause without any particular expression at all. And even if that's what they're told to do, they shouldn't act as if every news item is something extraordinary. And they shouldn't always try to look cheerful. You ought to modify your expression when you announce an earthquake, or a bomb attack in Lebanon, or a coach crash, or the death of a celebrity. But you're in such a hurry to get to the laughs you're already in fits over the coach crash. And if you do that you're in trouble. You start having sleepless nights. You don't know what you're saying any more. The television news bulletins are a riot from start to finish, and you have a nervous breakdown.

But on the whole, apart from the occasional major event such as the deaths of the famous, the Nobel Prize and votes in Parliament, nothing ever happens on television. No one ever speaks, really speaks, on it. I mean no one ever takes some minor news item like a dog accident as his starting point and uses it to trigger off the human imagination, our power to interpret the universe creatively; to awaken the strange genius so many of us have by means of a dog that got run over. Real talking has nothing to do with what happens on television. Though admittedly we customers, who buy TV sets and pay a tax for the privilege, look forward to slips of the tongue and suchlike, whether made by members of the government or journalists earning ten million francs a month. At the opening of the 1984 Book Fair, Chirac said he read poetry because as it's short it's the most convenient form of reading for someone who has to do a lot of flying. I once heard someone refer to *Hiroshima Mon Amour* as the famous film by Alain René and Jacqueline Duval. I've also heard someone talk about '*L'Amante Anglaise*, with the celebrated actress Madeleine Barrault'. Admittedly, this was a shy little girl who'd only just been taken on.

But perhaps if we heard real language being spoken on TV, by people who instead of play-acting were simply talking about current events between themselves, we shouldn't care for it at all. The news wouldn't be sufficiently odd or far-out; it would be too true. People sit in front of the television because it lies, of necessity, about both form and content. If journalists ever say exactly what we want them to, as they did during the miraculous students' strike in December 1986, we're afraid for them. We feel like kissing them and writing to them. Their contribution became part of the strike – and that's something that almost never happens. But it did happen in France in December 1986. Everyone in Paris was talking as much about that as about the strike itself. Those news bulletins were a real joy, until Pasqua and Pandraud unleashed their bloodhounds.

A WAY WITH WORDS

My mother was scared of people in office – civil servants, income tax inspectors, customs men, bailiffs, customs officers, anyone whose job it was to enforce the law. She always felt in the wrong – the typical, incurable attitude of the poor. She never entirely got over it. But I did, through oral exams. Every time I passed one I felt I'd made some progress against the poverty endemic to our family. A way with words. It was like a physical confrontation between me and society, there to try to destroy me. Singers and actors must go through the same experience with the audience. The people who pay to hear you sing or speak are enemies you have to get the better of in order to survive. But when you've done it once, after you've once mastered the words and carried the audience with you, it happens to you all the time. You pretend it's up to you not to disappoint the people who've gone to the trouble of coming to hear you. But there's more to it than that. Something that verges on wanting to kill the person who's come to sit in judgement on you.

THE GREEN STEAK

No, I've never been afraid of offending them. Everybody else I see around me seems afraid of it, of letting them down, but on the contrary, I want to offend them so that they'll know we're not all at their mercy. When you go to buy a steak and they keep showing you the 'good side', the red side, I say, 'I'd like to see the other side, please.' They always answer, 'I'll show you the other side of *this* one – they're both from the same cut.' And they put the first bit to one side, with the surface you're not supposed to see facing down. One day when I came out of hospital – another of my attacks of emphysema – I asked Yann to buy me a piece of steak. I felt like eating some meat. But Yann never likes to say anything to people in shops – he'd rather put up with anything, even food poisoning. So that day he came back with a steak that was green through being kept too long. I picked it up and showed it to him and said: 'Didn't you say anything?' And he said, 'No, I didn't like to.' I started to cry. I couldn't help it. I said: 'Listen, this is my first meal after I come out of hospital. You could have thrown it away and bought me another.' He said: 'I didn't think of it.' I didn't cry any more. I got hold of the steak and threw it in the dustbin. I was purple with rage. The steak was green and I was purple.

When he came back for dinner I took the steak out of the dustbin beforehand and put it on his plate. He took one look at it, gave a yell of horror, and threw it in the dustbin for good. It was never seen on a table again.

I've got another fad too, since we're on the subject. I always talk to the people sitting next to me, especially when I'm flying. I do it to make them say something back. If they answer it's because they feel safe, and that makes me feel safe too. I talk about the landscape or about travel in general, including flying. On the train I talk for talking's sake to complete strangers. I talk about what we can see, the countryside, the weather. I often feel like talking very fast and very loud.

Once, on a plane, I was sitting next to a man who wouldn't answer. Whatever I said to him, it wasn't any good. So I gave up. I thought he just didn't like the look of me. It didn't occur to me that he didn't know me. And as we were leaving he said, 'Goodbye, Marguerite Duras.' So I'd been right. He just didn't want to talk to me.

WON'T YOU?

To go back to what I was saying about the sexual desires aroused by writers, including even women novelists seventy years old, I wanted to tell you about this. About two or three years ago I received a letter from a man, the sort of letter that says, 'I'm coming to make love to you on Monday, 23 January, and I'll ring at the door at nine in the morning.' A lunatic, you think, and forget all about it. And on Monday, 23 January, at nine o'clock in the morning, there's a ring at the door. 'Who is it?' 'Me.' I say, 'You must be joking.' The other person says, 'Won't you?' I say, 'No, I won't.' He didn't say any more. He just lay down by the door. He stayed there all the morning. I phoned the people in the other flats; we're all very neighbourly and they know I'm sometimes in a spot. So they came and said to the young man, 'We know her(!) – she's never going to open the door, you know.' He said something charming, like: 'I'm all right where I am. At least I'm close to her.' I couldn't go out till early afternoon. He left without saying goodbye.

I'll tell you all: if anyone else had written *Lol V. Stein*, I don't know that I'd have accepted it very easily. The same with *The Vice-Consul* and *The War*. And *The Atlantic Man*. I'd either have given up writing or I'd have done a Rinaldi. Who knows?

What do I think about Sartre? I don't think anything about him most of the time. When I do I can't help comparing him with Solzhenitsyn. The Solzhenitsyn of a country without a Gulag. I see him as all alone in a wilderness created by himself. A kind of exile. I wish Conrad were still alive. How marvellous it would be to have a new Conrad novel every year.

My great craze in recent years hasn't been Proust, it's been Musil, especially *The Man without Qualities*, the last volume. If today, 20 September, I had to name the authors I've read with passion in the last few years, I'd say they were Ségalen and Musil. But, also on 20 September, the finest and most shattering thing I've read for years is Matisse on the Barnes Foundation ballet, in the collection *Ecrits et Propos sur l'Art* [Observations, written and spoken, on art], edited by the poet Dominique Fourcade and published by Hermann. I'm reading Renan at the moment – *The Life of Jesus* – and the Bible, and between whiles the marvellous dialogue in *The Mother and the Whore* by Jean Eustache. Are my books difficult? – is that what you want to know? Yes, they are difficult. And easy too. *The Lover* is very difficult. *The Malady of Death* is difficult, very difficult. *The Atlantic Man* is very difficult, but it's so fine it isn't difficult. Even if you don't understand it. You can't understand these books anyway. That's not the right word. It's a matter of a private relationship between the book and the reader. They weep and grieve together.

THE WATCHTOWERS AT POISSY

When I'm in Paris, writing, I miss the outside world, I miss being able to go out. None of the people round me have any idea how much. I can't write outside, but I need places not to write just as much as places to write. In Paris it's difficult for me to get out. I can't go out on my own – it's impossible. I can't walk far outside. I can't breathe properly. I *can* breathe and walk all right in the dark, empty corridors of the Black Rocks Hotel. For twenty years they've been telling me that what's wrong with me is emphysema. Sometimes, often, I believe it, but sometimes I don't. The attacks always happen when I leave my apartment – on the very landing. When I leave the building itself it's different again – it's as if I were entering an outside that's cut off from inside by a knife. As if I were entering *into* the street, a street that's harshly lit and like a huge cage, at once the outside and something that closes you in. It reminds me of the spaces lit up by the watchtowers of prisons, in particular those of the old prison at Poissy, which I've often driven past. The ground is evenly lit up all over without any shadow; there's nowhere for a body to be. I'm quite prepared to believe what's wrong with me is emphysema. As soon as I get into my car and shut the door, I'm saved. From what? From you, the people I write for, who recognize me wherever I go, even in the street. I can't get over the terror that seizes me when I enter that open, sunny place of public execution. When I'm submerged in it. I mean the street, the pedestrian crossings, the squares, the city. Just going out, as most people do, to stroll about and look at what's going on – for years and years that's been a thing of the past for me. I'll never be like those people, like you, again. But I have found the solution of the car. So long as I've got the car I can go on. So long as I can drive around and look at the Seine, look at Normandy, I can go on. After that, I don't know. When no one wants to come out for a drive with me any more, I don't know what I'll do. This October I went to Paris and came back the next day all on my own. It isn't that driving tires me, but I find it difficult driving for a long time on my own. I can't manage to talk to myself, even once in five hundred kilometres. So I'd rather be shut up in the apartment than drive long distances alone. Another thing is that I can't go down into the underground garage to fetch the car or put it away. I'm terrified of underground garages. In the same way, I can't drive if anyone looks at me or recognizes me. It's the alcohol. And the terrible cure. 'Sometimes you'll have experiences you'll recognize, as if you'd been drinking again. But it'll pass,' the doctor said. And he was right.

Once out on the road I feel safe, and I can drive well and fast.

My son's here at Trouville, and he just said, 'You've taken up all the tables in the apartment again.' It's quite true. And when they don't want to come for drives with me any more, when they won't let me take up all the tables in the apartment any more, I don't know what I'll do. I know the time will come; it's inevitable. It's probably already there, already begun.

At Trouville the sea's always there. Night and day, even if you can't see it, the thought of it's there. In Paris only windy and stormy days link us to the sea. Otherwise we're bereft of it.

Here we're part of the same landscape.

Beyond every hill there's that great emptiness in the distance. Over every hill the sky is different, hollower, lighter. More resonant, you might say. And it's true the gulls make less noise in the city than they do over the water, over the beaches.

I can bear to live in Trouville. But not in Paris, I must admit. Because of the threatening spaces, the open streets, and the people who come ringing at the door, from a long way away, from Germany – often from Germany, actually. They ring at the door and they come just so as to have seen me.

'What is it, please?'

'We'd like to see Madame Duras.'

They want to talk to me, and about me, as if my time belonged to them, as if it was my job to talk to them about myself. Those people are you, whom I love and for whom I write.

It's you that frighten me, you who are sometimes just as terrifying as gangsters.

THE VASTY DEEP

In my street they're currently demolishing a big printing press that was built in the nineteenth century. The press where they printed the *Journal Officiel*. As the outside is listed, they're just knocking down the inner walls. I apologize for the noise you can hear in the book – the sound of pneumatic drills, and above all the crash of the great blocks of stone on chains that they use to knock the inside walls down with. And the shouts of the Arab workmen clearing everyone out before the chains go into action. It's going to be a three-star hotel. The name's wrong: 'Latitudes', as if it were on the Mediterranean. All the printing workers have gone. Never again shall we know the magnificent throb, strong yet gentle and harmless, of the great rotary presses that we used to hear every morning, and sometimes at night too when there was a special session of Parliament. They're going to add two extra floors. The press itself didn't come up as far as our floor; it stopped at the second. From Yann's room you could look through a courtyard and see the time on the clock of Saint-Germain-des-Prés. But that's all over. Since Friday, 18 December 1986 the view of the clock has been hidden by a breeze-block wall. The hotel will take up half the block between the rue Saint-Benôit and the rue Bonaparte. The style of the façade is reminiscent of the department stores on downtown Broadway. Fluted bronze columns and charming angels. The hotel opens in the spring of 1987. Three hundred bedrooms. Three stars. And called 'Latitudes'. Why not 'The Vasty Deep'? It gives you an idea of the philistinism of the property promoters. They're in the middle of the 6th arrondissement and they name their hotel as if it were some cheap modern place in the Languedoc. It's Bouygues' doing. It's both unpronounceable and meaningless. You might think it has a meaning, but it hasn't. For fifty years he made cement-mixers, and now all of a sudden he builds a hotel. You can't help feeling sorry for him.

PARIS

Here the sea is a protection against asphyxiation, against being buried in the town. Here Paris seems a blunder, the kind of city that shouldn't be allowed to exist. Paris is where you find the market in death, the market in sex and drugs. It's there that old ladies get murdered. It's there that people set fire to immigrants' hostels – six in two years. It's there that there's a special race of motorists who don't know how to behave, who are coarse and insulting and use their cars to kill with. The *nouveaux riches* of the financial world, the managing directors of death, zooming about in Volvos and BMWs. They used to be the sort of cars that stood for elegance in other things as well – elegant shoes and perfume, elegant voices with a courteous word for everyone. Snobbery, but in a discreet form. Now you wouldn't want to buy that sort of car any more. Paris has become a kind of medina. You get lost in it. An ideal place for protecting, covering up and absorbing crime – a monster molecule made up of twelve million inhabitants. A crime like the murder of Georges Besse the other day is unimaginable anywhere but in Paris, inside the protecting walls of human concrete. Its disorder has become its ramparts. Disorder sets its seals on the suburbs one concentric circle after another. It's all happened in twenty

years. The disorder is crossed and served by networks of
motorways which lead to the international airports. There
aren't any road maps for the suburbs any more; it's impossible
to keep up to date with any but the main arteries. The wooded
areas in and around Paris have a bad reputation. The Bois de
Boulogne belongs to prostitutes and the police at night,
and in the daytime to drug dealers. So what's left for us
'respectable' people? It's in Paris that foreigners come off the
worst. The food is worse there than anywhere else in France.
The 6th arrondissement, a ravishingly beautiful centre of
French culture visited by intellectuals from all over the world,
is notorious as one of the places where it's hardest to find a
good restaurant. The food in most of them, as in all tourist
haunts, is mass-produced; the two or three exceptions include
the Brasserie Lipp and Le Petit Saint-Benôit. Don't let's even
speak of the Asian restaurants and their moggy pâté. The
poor little Asian cats! Paris is also the place with the most
dogs, but that doesn't matter, seeing we don't eat *them*.
Something has happened to this city. What? Is it the motorcar?
I'm inclined to think so. Or else it's that slacking at school
has been carried over into real life long enough to affect
several generations. Perhaps through neglecting their studies
people got to understand less and less, until finally they didn't
understand anything at all. And afterwards they didn't know
how to live. And then they ran away. We didn't believe in
school, at any level. We behaved badly. We forgot all we'd
learned, all our politeness, all our subtlety, all our wit. And
all that's left is business know-how.

About ten years ago the suburbs of Paris had twelve million
inhabitants. It's a long time now since I saw any official

figures. Perhaps they've lost count of the number of people who live there. Perhaps it's a floating population that lives in hiding places rather than homes. What with drugs and robbery and terrorism, the suburbs must support about as many people as a provincial town. The largest section consists of people without any occupation, without work or home, family or papers; no one will take responsibility for them for fear of their past; they're abandoned, lost, like the street children in Mexico. All the food they get is what they can steal from supermarkets. The only way they can get clothes or shoes is by theft. The only way they can get a coffee or a cigarette is from one another. They've already developed a mixed colour from never mind what racial ingredients. Frizzy black curls, black eyes. They're tall and handsome, and they'll be the front runners in the unemployment crises foretold in *Green Eyes*. There they are. Stagnating. Doing nothing. Except be alive. And watch. You can see them hanging about in the television stores, the métros, the railway stations and the shopping malls of Créteil-Soleil.

Paris can't move any more, can't expand at a normal rate. And it has lost the significance it once had. But people still come here in the hope of getting closer to meaning, to what they expect to find in a capital city, which is made up of the essence of every kind of knowledge, from the arts of building, writing and painting to that of politics. If you ask someone who lives in the suburbs he'll say: 'I used to live in Chartres or Rambouillet, but in the end I got bored and came to Paris to be nearer.' Just for that. But he can't say nearer to what. Yet this inability, which is usually permanent, is perhaps what really gets closest to the meaning of life, in every sense of the word. People come to Paris, to the capital, to give their lives a sense of belonging, of an almost mythical participation in society. Once outside the northern gates of Paris you come to the windswept settlements that stretch from Saint-Denis to La Courneuve and on to Sarcelles. To the south, thanks to the miraculous enclave formed by the Château of Versailles, you reach the fields sooner – the forests, the byeways, the village squares. But the real meaning of it all, the most important, is Paris.

No one can ever describe the beauty of Paris all the year round – from Sundays in summer to winter nights when the streets become primitive again, like roads. No other city in the world is constructed like Paris, with its incredible wealth of open spaces. Part of it rivals Versailles in the number of its great public buildings. It's in summer that the river emerges in all its beauty, with its shady trees, its gardens, the great avenues lining or radiating from it, the gentle slopes overlooking it on all sides, from the Etoile and from Montparnasse, Montmartre and Belleville. The only flat parts are around Concorde and the Louvre, and on the islands.

THE RED SOFA

I moved into this apartment in April 1942 and it's now February 1987, so I shall soon have lived here for forty-five years. In that time I've slept in three out of the five rooms. When my son was small I let him have what is now my bedroom so that he'd have more space. Once, in the bedroom overlooking the courtyard – the room where we kept coal when it was rationed during the war – I made a discovery. In broad daylight, though. And I was alone. It was inside a cupboard built directly on to the wooden floor. The strips of wood were coming apart, so I pushed them back together, but one of them wouldn't lie flat, and underneath I found some real tortoise-shell hairpins and a hand-made louse-comb of chalk-white bone. The teeth of the comb were as fine as linen threads, and at the base of some of them were tiny shadows – nits, perhaps, or lice, that had got caught. Apart from that, nothing. The apartment has stayed the same as when I first rented it, standing here stable and unchanging in the rue Saint-Benôit. But it did change once in all these years – one fortnight after my drying-out treatment. It seemed to me it had twisted round on a central axis. The windows had moved, and the walls went in different directions. It was no longer quite the same apartment, or rather it was the same apartment only turned round on itself. But the strangest thing about it was the logic, the mathematical rigour of the shift. All the windows and doors had moved through just the number of degrees necessary for everything to remain the same in itself but different in relation to the central axis. Not one detail had moved too much or too little. Nothing had been forgotten or left out; the change had been carried out with the accuracy of an architect's drawing. Even the right angle where the bathroom walls meet had become slightly acute. The same thing was repeated exactly outside. All that I could see out of the windows overlooking the courtyard was similarly displaced. But it was difficult to see everything. There were balconies now along the roofs.

There were some new pieces of furniture too – some that I'd known years ago and thought I'd forgotten, and others I'd never seen before. There were also some people I'd never seen before – the people who'd bought my apartment. They were merchants from Judaea dressed in gallabiyas, and they were sitting on a red sofa which really had existed in the past. But now it was in the wrong place, in front of my bedroom fireplace, waiting, as I believed, to be moved to a better position. I had to find out what that position was.

These things didn't all disappear in one night. The first one to go was the red sofa. It belonged to a friend of mine, Georgette de Cormis, who'd left it with me to look after during the war. She lived in Aix-en-Provence, and had taken it back again some time between 1950 and 1955.

THE ROUND STONES

One day I found a round stone with some straight grooves
marked on it – a triangle with a line through. It had been left
on top of the dustbin by some Portuguese workmen who'd
come to repair the walls of the cellar. I found out afterwards
that they'd put it there purposely in case anyone might be
interested in it. I carried it up and put it on my kitchen table,
then went downstairs again because I thought I'd seen another
one. And sure enough there was another round stone, with
more definite marks this time: it had a hole through the
middle and a notch on one side, both obviously made by
hand. Parallel to the notch was a grooved slot, probably to
take a now vanished wooden tongue. The first stone was in
its original form except for a small patch that had been
polished to take the signature. The second had been completely reshaped. It fitted exactly over the other stone, and
then they would both revolve. I sat looking at them all night.
They were from the cellars of the abbey of Saint-Laurent,
which used to stretch down as far as the banks of the Seine.
One day I showed them to Michel Leiris, but he didn't know
what they could have been for either. He thought they might
have been for crushing grain or fruit to extract oil; the oil

would have run out through the opening at the side. But it wasn't certain. I remembered the plague, and washed them, to be on the safe side.

THE CHEST OF DRAWERS

It was a rustic Louis Quinze chest of drawers I'd got from an antique shop in the 6th arrondissement – I must have been about thirty-five or forty at the time, and I probably bought it with the money I got for *The Sea Wall*. I'd had it for about ten years or so when one night I was tidying my things, as lots of women do, and for some reason I don't remember now I took the middle drawer out and put it on the floor. And a piece of material that had been caught between the drawer and the back of the commode fell out of the shadows. It was a slightly yellowish white, but bright, crumpled like a screwed-up piece of paper, and flecked with pale pink stains. It was a caraco, a woman's loose under-blouse, gathered at the neck and with a narrow lace trimming round the edge. It was made of lawn. It had been there since the days of the chest of drawers' first owners. No one had ever taken the drawers out, even when moving house. 'Seventeen twenty,' I said aloud. The pink marks were like those made by the light-coloured blood of the last days of menstruation. The caraco must have been put away after it had been washed: it was spotlessly clean apart from the marks, which would only come out in the big annual wash. The pink of the marks was the colour blood leaves on cloth after it has been rinsed. The caraco itself had taken on the smell of polished wood. The drawer must have been too full, and the under-blouse, on top, must have got caught and dragged by the drawer above until it disappeared down the back of the commode. And there it stayed for two hundred years. It was covered with months and years of darns – with darns which had been darned themselves, as beautiful as embroidery. The first thing you think when you realize what it is, is: 'She must have hunted for it all over the place.' For days and nights. She couldn't think where it could have got to.

WASTING TIME

It's very mysterious, what a woman does with her time at the distance I am from my youth. It's very frightening as well. Your own case is always the worst. Life is only lived full-time by women with children. Children give them certainty. They're overwhelmed by the demands children make – their bodies, their beauty, the care you have to lavish on them, the undivided love each one of them requires and without which they die. Women with their children is the only thing you can look at without feeling depressed. Apart from that, at the distance I am from you, just as at the distance you all are from one another, all lives seem completely meaningless and without *raison d'être*. Every life is an insoluble problem. All the people piled up on top of one another in blocks of flats – you ask yourself how it's possible, and yet you're one of the layers.

The best way to fill time is to waste it.

It's not so painful even to contemplate all the young people hanging around outside churches and public places, in TV stores or around the Forum des Halles, waiting for something to happen, as it is to look at the workers, piled up in layers in the giant housing schemes on the outskirts of Paris, woken up by the alarm on a winter's morning while it's still dark. To go to work just so as to stay alive.

THE CHIMNEYS OF *INDIA SONG*

One day, if I live to be very old, I'll stop writing. And no doubt it will seem to me unreal, impossible, absurd.

One day I thought it had happened – that I'd never write again. It was during that drying-out treatment. I remember it well. It was in the American Hospital. I was standing at the window, leaning on Yann's arm. I was looking at the red roofs opposite, and at the fair-haired woman with blue eyes who was sticking up out of the chimney. Her husband, the captain in *India Song*, was looking distractedly at the sky. He was emerging from another chimney. Suddenly I started to cry. It was quite clear to me: as I told Yann, I'd probably never write anything any more. It was all over. I really believed it, and I can still remember the terrible grief I felt. But it didn't get rid of the apparitions in the chimneys. They just watched me grieving.

When I came home from the American Hospital I tried straight away to write something in my engagement book. Physically, I mean – I just tried to hold the pen and write. At first I couldn't form the letters, and then it all came back. But where did this new, temporary writing come from? It was like the hole underneath the house when they heightened the step. It was the writing of a five-year-old child – irregular, smudged. Like the writing of a criminal, why not.

I'd like to write a book the way I'm writing at this moment, the way I'm talking to you at this moment. I'm scarcely conscious of the words coming out of me. Nothing seems to be being said but the almost nothing there is in all words.

You never know, in life, when things are there. You can't grasp them. You were saying the other day that life often seems as if it were dubbed. That's exactly what I feel: my life is a film that's been dubbed – badly cut, badly acted, badly put together. In short, a mistake. A whodunnit without either murders or cops or victims; without a subject; pointless. It could have been a real film, but no, it's a sham. But who's to say what one would have had to do for it to be otherwise? I suppose I should have just stood there in front of the camera without saying or doing anything; just being looked at, without thinking about anything in particular. Yes, that's it.

It's only late in life that you start drawing conclusions from your experience. You'll see. I mean, that you dare to say or write them. So it's afterwards you realize that the feeling of happiness you had with a man didn't necessarily prove that you loved him. Now I find evidence of love in memories less strong and less articulate. It was the men I deceived the most that I loved the most.

There's a comedy of love that sometimes – often – perhaps usually – applies to every couple. I've changed my mind about this, too. A great deal. Most people stay together because together they're not so frightened. Or because it's easier to live on two salaries than on one. Or because of the children. Or for lots of other reasons that they never really go into but which show that a choice has been made, even if it's an irrational one, and a definite position taken up, even if it's difficult or impossible to put into words. 'You couldn't understand,' they say. Or, 'I don't know myself what makes me stay, but I can't do anything else.' These aren't people who love one another, but it is love that's between them just the same. Loving someone for this reason or that, out of practical considerations or convenience, is still love. People don't usually talk about it – they may not even be aware of it – but it is love. It's the kind of love that's revealed by death. Sometimes one's horrified by certain couples: the man's brutish and coarse, and the woman tells anyone who cares to listen that she's going through hell. But one can be wrong about such people. Theirs is a kind of play-acting love, but it's often a mistake to think it has nothing to do with the real thing. When Bernard Pivot asked me what made me stay with the Chinese lover, I said: 'Money.' But I might also have said it was the fabulous luxury of the car, which was more like a salon. The chauffeur. Having the car and the chauffeur at my disposal. The sexual smell of the silk tussore, and of his, the lover's, skin. They conditioned me to love, if you like. I really started to love him after I'd left him, probably just when I heard of the suicide of the young man who was lost at sea. I must have found out then, in the middle of the voyage. I think love always goes with love: you can't just love by yourself – I don't believe in that. I don't believe in hopeless love affairs concerning only one person. He loved me so much I had to love him; he desired me so much I had to desire him. But it's not possible to love someone who doesn't see anything attractive in you at all, who finds you completely boring. I don't believe in that, either.

THE VOICE IN *NAVIRE NIGHT*

In *Navire Night* it's the voice that acts, that produces desire and emotion. The voice is stronger than physical presence. It's as important as the face, the eyes, the smile. A real letter is moving because it's spoken, written with the spoken voice. I get letters that make me fall in love with the people who wrote them. But of course one can't reply.

I did reply to Yann. I began by seeing him, when *India Song* was shown in Caen. A group of us went to a café afterwards. At first, to Yann, I was the person who'd written *India Song*, who'd made Anne-Marie Stretter speak about the boredom in India. Michael Richardson, Lol V. Stein, the beggar woman – to begin with I was all these people to Yann, and it was because of them that he came to Trouville. After he began reading the books he'd come under a sort of spell and written to me. As in the other cases, I hadn't replied. And then one day I did. I remember that day very clearly. The only thing I wanted to do was to write to the young student I'd met in Caen and tell him how difficult I was finding it to go on living. I told him I drank a lot, that I'd been in hospital because of it, and that I didn't know why I drank so much.

It happened in January 1980. I was seventy. You, Jérôme Beaujour, were there when it happened. I had very high blood pressure and had been prescribed anti-depressants, but I hadn't told the doctor I was an alcoholic. As a result I had several blackouts a day for three days. I was taken to hospital in Saint-Germain-en-Laye in the middle of the night. And so on. It was after I came out that I wrote to Yann, a man I didn't know, because of the letters he'd written to me. I've kept them; they're wonderful. And then one day, seven months later, he phoned and asked if he could come. It was summer. Just listening to the sound of his voice I knew it was madness. But I told him to come. He left his home and his job. And he stayed. That was six years ago now.

EATING AT NIGHT

I buy him cheese and yoghourt and butter in Trouville, because when he comes in late at night he devours that sort of thing. And he buys me the things I like best – buns and fruit. He buys them not so much to give me pleasure as to feed me up. He has this childlike idea of making me eat so that I don't die. He doesn't want me to die. But he doesn't want me to get fat either. It's hard to reconcile the two. I don't want to die, either. That's what our affection is like; our love. In the evening and at night, talking, we sometimes throw caution to the winds. In these conversations we tell the truth however terrible, and we laugh as we used to do when we still drank and could only talk to one another in the afternoon.

OCTOBER 1982

Instead of drinking coffee when I woke up, during the last few months I started straight away on whisky or wine. I was often sick after the wine – the pituitary vomiting typical of alcoholics. I'd vomit the wine I'd just drunk, and start drinking some more right away. Usually the vomiting stopped after the second try, and I'd be glad. Yann used to drink in the morning too, but less than me, I think. No, he didn't drink as much as I did.

He drank the evening he came to Trouville in August 1980, and he went on drinking until I went into the American Hospital. He'd put on weight too. I don't know why he drank with me; at the same time as I did. I don't think he saw I was dying. I seem to remember it was someone else who told him – Michèle Manceau, perhaps: 'You don't see it, but she's dying.'

She called in a friend of hers, a Jew from Moldavia – love and greetings, Daniel – but I think some time still went by after that. He wanted me to make my own decision and state it quite clearly.

Every day Yann asked me to fix the date, and one day I did. I said: 'October.' The beginning of October 1982.

They phoned and booked a room.

It still frightens me to write the words: October, the beginning of October.

Daniel had warned me. He'd said: 'I must tell you – it'll be very tough. But you have no choice. You'll never lick this on your own, you know.' I knew.

So I'd been warned the cure would be tough. But I really had nothing to judge by, as I realize now. If you could know in advance what the American cure called 'cold turkey' is really like, you could never bring yourself to undergo it, you'd never coolly choose a date for it. No, you'd run away.

It was when we were in the taxi and I saw Daniel hurry away, weeping, that I realized I'd let myself in for something from which there was no turning back. I'd drunk a lot that day. It had all been rather vague up till then, and I'd laughed at the others for their apprehensions. But there in the taxi I could see Yann's fear growing and becoming tense and terrible. My legs had suddenly swelled up too, and that had frightened us, though we didn't know why.

At eight o'clock in the evening I found myself alone in a room in the American Hospital. They'd asked Yann not to stay. I'm writing very fast – I'm sorry. I don't know if you can follow the order of events. Never mind.

There's one thing that has stayed with me, the most important one – the fear of doing it again. The cure, I mean. I know it only hangs by a hair – one sip of alcohol, a sweet flavoured with rum. Just before Yann came to Trouville I'd noticed in passing, not thinking anything of it, that there was still a drop of vermouth left in a bottle in the hall cupboard which I'd thought was empty. I thought about it a couple of days later, and then every evening of every day for a week or ten days.

And then I drank it. After that Yann came and I told him to buy some wine; and that was it. That was the third time I'd started again. Now I'm in my third non-drinking period. As I've already told you.

The evening I went into the American Hospital I was relying on pills to make me sleep, but at four o'clock in the morning I was still awake. And suddenly I thought, 'There isn't any drink in the room.' And I was frightened. I hastily thought of a plan to forestall the coma I knew was inevitable: I'd phone for a taxi and go to the Porte Maillot, ask the taxi to wait while I bought a bottle of red wine in a bar, and bring it back to the hospital without anyone being any the wiser. I got up and dressed quietly. Then suddenly there stood a nurse, who'd come in without my hearing her. I shouted at her: 'You know I could fall into a coma!' She said: 'But there's some wine here, Madame. I'll give you a glass.' They'd expected this to happen. That was my last drink. October 1982.

You must always see to it that you don't have anything dangerous within reach. I know the least thing could start me off again.

A DANGEROUS STATE

At present I blame myself for writing: it's always like this after I've finished a book. And if it means falling into my present state afterwards, writing isn't worth the candle. If I can't do it without being in danger of drinking again, it's just not worthwhile. That's what I say to myself sometimes, as if I could help it. That's a dangerous state too.

Don't take any notice of what I said the last time about the cure. One could start again, cure or no cure. This evening. Just like that. For no other reason than that one's an alcoholic.

LETTERS

I myself wrote letters once, as Yann did to me – for two years, to someone I'd never met. Then Yann came. He took the place of the letters. It's impossible to do without love altogether. Even if words are all that's left, it's still real. The worst is not to love at all. I don't think that's possible.

THE PEOPLE OF THE NIGHT

I handed *The Lover* in to the Editions de Minuit in June 1984. Then I made the film, then I cut it, and then I wrote *The War*. Then I fell ill. The day *The War* came out, I was in hospital. Yann brought me the article by Poirot-Delpech, but I was on artificial respiration. Again I was out of my mind for a week; as also in April 1985. I nearly killed a young nurse. The whole scenario was very clear. On the one hand that evening there was Yann, who'd gone home and to whom I'd given my rings. On the other hand there was a young night nurse, who'd advised me to give the rings to Yann so that they wouldn't get stolen. I'd told her I'd taken her advice, and that Yann had taken the rings back to my place, where he lived. At midnight the nurse, who was supposed to come in and see to me, still hadn't come. I waited for her till three or four in the morning. And then madness struck, with the irrefutable explanation: the nurse, with some of her so-called colleagues, had gone to the rue Saint-Benôit to kill Yann and take my rings.

When it got light I opened the window of my room and shouted out that I was going to be murdered and someone must come. Nothing happened, though I was told later that people had heard me. I yelled again. Implored. Nothing.

In the morning, when the nurse came back, I was hiding under a sheet with a knife I'd brought from home. She shouted for help. I shouted again too – I said my life was in danger, I was being murdered. A nursing auxiliary came. He was horrified. He leapt on me and took away the knife – wounding me in the process.

I think that was how I 'knew' I'd been kidnapped by the so-called 'doctors' at the hospital. For hours, apparently, I kept telling them how they could get a ransom. I told them whom to phone and how much to ask. I suggested quite a low figure. About what I thought I was worth on the murder market.

I've forgotten all those ravings, but what impresses me still is the logic, the cogency of the argument about the murder and the rings. It was so obvious that I was convinced it must be true.

This is what happens when you have a bad attack of emphysema: your brain doesn't get enough oxygen and your mind goes. The week before me they'd had a young man who refereed an imaginary football match for a whole afternoon. Then they put him on an oxygen machine and it was all over. The doctors found this sort of thing very amusing. But it still terrifies me. It's frightening when people tell you about things you've said or done that you don't remember. I remember practically nothing about the alcoholic delusions I had during the cure. I was in a kind of coma when I had them, and I only emerged occasionally, for a few seconds. On the other hand I can remember quite clearly the things I saw after the cure. They started while I was still in the American Hospital.

India Song had become a boat. I've told you this before, but never mind. The captain's wife lived on the roof opposite, sticking up out of a funnel or chimney. She was fair and pink, with blue eyes. Only her head emerged from the funnel. The captain was a couple of yards away in the same position as his wife: stuck in a funnel or chimney. One day it was very windy, and the wife's head shattered as if it had been made of glass. I was scandalized. *Exactly* ten thousand tortoises were arranged round the roof like books on shelves. When it got dark they went back under the eaves. All these images were brighter than reality, as if lit up from within. It took the tortoises several hours to huddle together and settle down for the night. I was shocked that nature should be so inefficient. They took so long to sort themselves out that a lot of them just had to stay where they were.

Among these 'memories' there's a kind of Asian mandarin all dressed up in blue and gold brocade. He used to roam about the hospital corridors, impassive, taciturn, and very frightening. I'm not sure if it was at Laennec or the American Hospital. No one else seemed to see him. Perhaps he didn't exist. In the American Hospital I could see Michael Richardson through the closed, uncurtained windows of the house in *India Song*. He was surrounded by plants and creepers. He smiled and wept at the same time, imprisoned in the story. Very handsome. The famous black Abyssinian cow, all skin and bones, was leaning against the wall by the front door. Beside her stood a big red and gold chair. Both were like the sort of thing you see chucked out and abandoned on the pavement in Neuilly. And some evenings Michael Lonsdale would be there, sitting in a corner dressed as a Bedouin and smiling at me.

After I'd gone home the most amazing delusions used to

occur at night. The sound of singing, solo and in chorus, would rise up from the inner courtyard under my windows. And when I looked out I would see crowds of people who I was sure had come to save me from death. Some of them carried pikes with shrivelled heads on top. They talked about someone, a child apparently, whom they referred to as 'little Gauthier'. I remember someone on the stairs in the middle of the night, calling out softly and with unforgettable tenderness: 'If they hurt little Gauthier I shall die.'

There were a number of us living in the apartment then. In the bathroom there was a woman behind the toilet, holding a dead child wrapped up in white bandages. She was there so patently that in the end I stopped taking any notice. There were men too, five of them, who used to come into Yann's room at night. These were *real* men, who walked and talked. Their bodies were stuffed with crumpled newspaper. There were animals under my table, and the famous dwarfs with pigs' tails, that we called 'lamias'. There was also a bust of a woman in painted terracotta – the French Republic – on a little shelf by my desk.

Above all there was the terrifying man who lived near Yann's room and spied on me. I was deafened all the time by telephone calls. I'd discovered that the exchange was in a maid's room, used by my enemies, on the sixth floor on the other side of the courtyard. My neighbour opposite had stolen my line. I knew it and I could prove it. The ringings formed a circle round my bedroom, and that didn't seem normal. But strangest of all were the scenes that took place every day inside the apartment. The dead dog hung up behind my radiator, for example. Though I wasn't sure if it wasn't at the same time a bird. A blue duck. I was under the impression I didn't sleep for days. But I didn't feel tired. In a way I never woke up.

It started with rats and other animals. The place was suddenly overrun with them in the middle of one night. Yann heard the commotion: I had my shoes on and was chasing the rats with an umbrella. That's how it began. Oh, and I was forgetting – all this went on to the accompaniment of music from Wagner's operas. And yelling from the German police. And then there were the things Yann described in *M.D.* – the scenes where the Jews were being shot outside my windows. And then there were the Black women in the sitting room ... But I can't catalogue the whole horde of them. To give you a general idea: while the Jews and the Blacks were voluntarily swearing allegiance to the Nazis in the sitting room, my Moldavian doctor's friends were sitting in my bedroom on the red sofa – it hadn't been there the day before – preparing to buy the apartment, which the doctor himself must therefore have stolen. All day long, in the middle of this chaos, cats that only I could see prowled back and forth through the flat.

Reality returned quite suddenly. I can remember clearly a purée flavoured with nutmeg that Michèle Manceau had made for me. I devoured it. It was after that that the intruders gradually went away. The German police left the neighbouring balconies; the paper men disappeared from Yann's room. The man in my son's room was still there – the one with curly grey hair, a floury white face and staring wild blue eyes. There were a few cats left too. I think the last to go was Marianne – perhaps the most incredible and ridiculous thing of all, with her Lorraine cap. A shameful, patriotic object – God knows what she thought she was doing on the little shelf in my bedroom. Except that a week ago – we're now the beginning of April 1987 – I saw the same bust of Marianne in an apartment in the rue Bonaparte which overlooks the same courtyard as we do. I thought I'd never seen the bust before. But I recognized it as the one in the hallucination. It was now standing on a mantelpiece, and framed by an open window. The doctor said I'd remember everything in time. He said all the things in my delirium were real memories, things I'd seen or experienced. But so far I've traced only one. Sometimes, at night, I'm still afraid they might come back. It's impossible to imagine that you can see something when there's nothing there. But you can – right down to reality's last detail. The colour of someone's eyes, their hair, their skin. I recognized music by Wagner that I didn't even know. I told Yann, 'If this goes on for a couple of weeks I'll kill myself, I shan't be able to help it.' But why was it so unbearable? So unbearable that as the days went by it took away every reason for going on living? I think it must be because you're the only person who sees what you see, and all you're used to is being the only one who thinks what you think. Suddenly your brain lights up and becomes visible. You can see your own thoughts written up in large letters on a screen. But you know no one believes you. Even about the cats, which I tried to smuggle through by referring to them as if their presence was quite natural. And then you realize that it's soon going to be unbearable for the people who love you, and that they're going to have to part from you. The doctor had said I needed to have a lot of people around me all the time, people I didn't know too. But sooner or later I always had to go back alone into my room, to switch on the light and find the animals had got there again before me, the little pigs under the table and Marianne on the bookshelf. The doctor hadn't prescribed any tranquillizers; I found that rather strange, and so did my friends. All those creatures were supposed to leave me of their own accord. Not only were they not being kept out – they weren't even being urged to go.

I forgot to tell you that when I asked Yann to take the dead dog, the one the Nazis had killed, down from behind the radiator, I told him to throw it down hard out of the window on to the passers-by, so that they'd know some Jews had been murdered. I listened to what he was doing. It didn't seem to have taken him very long to unhook the dog and throw it out of the window, but that didn't make me doubt that the dead dog was real. What did make me doubt was Michèle Porte, one day. I was in the kitchen and she hung her coat up as she came in. We chatted for a while, and I told her about how I'd been seeing things. She listened, but didn't say anything. I said, 'I believe in them myself, but I can't convince anyone else.' Then I said, 'Turn round and look at your right-hand coat pocket. Do you see the little new-born puppy crawling out of it, all pink? Well, the others say I'm wrong and it's not really there.' She had a good look, then turned back to me. She gazed at me for some time, then said quite seriously, without a trace of a smile: 'Marguerite, I swear to you by all I hold dear that I don't see anything.' But she didn't say it wasn't there; she only said she couldn't see it. Perhaps that incident shows that even in madness there's a certain amount of reason.

And then one night I called Yann to throw out the man with the curly hair and the talcum-powdered face, who was now in the hall, only a couple of yards from my room. I heard a furious yell and then along came Yann, beside himself with anger and fatigue. Every night I was attacked by the 'people' lurking in the apartment and woke him up. 'Get it into your head that I can't see anything,' he yelled. 'Do you hear? There's nothing there! Nothing! Nothing!' I hid behind my bedroom door, because while Yann was yelling I'd seen the man with curly hair come up beside him, and I implored Yann to send him away. Then Yann didn't say any more.

The man – he was wearing a black overcoat – didn't understand what was going on. He moved a few steps closer to Yann. Then stopped. He was looking at me all the time. It was me he was interested in – and so passionately that it turned him absolutely and horribly pale. He looked at me with a kind of pained indignation: how was it *I* didn't look at *him*, but only wept and tried to get away from him? He didn't understand how I didn't understand what he wanted. It was as if he were someone I ought to recognize, but didn't. Even as I write this, three years later, I'm still worried about him. Either he wanted to take me away somewhere, not necessarily to death. Or else he was there to remind me of some immemorial connection which had been severed, but which had been my *raison d'être* ever since I was born. He was either a Jew or my father. Or something else. Someone else, indefinitely. But he himself was definite enough. He'd been here for a fortnight without changing. He lived here. For the last fortnight he'd been living in the little room overlooking the street. He had small very blue eyes, and very curly hair partly black and partly white, from another world, from another age. Yes, he knew something about me that I couldn't know. Not something I'd forgotten – something I ought to know. He was there then, mingled with the other apparitions, but central to them all. It was around him, the master apparition, that the other apparitions turned. And turned around my life. He didn't understand why I was afraid of him. He could see I was afraid, but he didn't know it was him I was afraid of; he didn't know what it was. I went on shouting at Yann to send him away, send him away. Then I discovered something terrible: he didn't understand French. He didn't understand what I was saying to Yann. His lips were slightly mauve, and sealed. He never spoke; he hadn't said a word for a fortnight. He must have thought he didn't have to tell me why he'd been there all those days and nights. He must have thought I knew why he was waiting for me. If I didn't understand it was because I didn't want to. He thought it was impossible for me not to know. But I couldn't know. The look in his eyes was frank and open right to the end: I must understand. But I couldn't.

Yann went to the front door. I went back into my room so as not to see. He opened the front door and then shut it again. He said, 'You can come out – he's gone.' And he had gone. Yann put his arms round me, and I wept for a long time.

I've never told anyone about this until now. It's as if something happened between that vision and me, something that lasted only a few seconds but was like the beginning of a shared knowledge. I can remember quite clearly the remote feeling of guilt that came to me after he'd gone, when Yann and I were alone again. As if I ought to have spoken to him. Ought to have explained that I couldn't act any differently because I didn't understand what he wanted of me.